GW00739295

FROST
anatomy of a success

Also by Wallace Reyburn

FROST
anatomy of a success

Wallace Reyburn

FIRST PUBLISHED IN 1968 BY
MACDONALD & CO. (PUBLISHERS) LTD.
49 POLAND STREET, LONDON, W. 1

© WALLACE REYBURN 1968

SBN 356 02496 2

PRINTED AND BOUND IN ENGLAND BY
HAZELL WATSON AND VINEY LTD
AYLESBURY, BUCKS

Contents

F.—I*

TO

the Rev. W. J. Paradine Frost

List of Plates

8 LIST OF PLATES

Chapter 1

The Frost Syndrome

The main picture on the front page of the *Methodist Recorder* of 30 November 1967, was a photograph of David Frost. On the same page was another picture of him in a quarter-page advertisement. On page three was a lengthy story about his activities. On page fourteen there was another picture of him. It was very much the David Frost issue of the *Recorder*.

But hidden away on page two was a little story headed "Death of the Rev. W. J. Paradine Frost". Four paragraphs outlined his forty years of dedicated work for the Methodist Church.

Of this Frost said, "I would so much have liked it to have been the other way round."

One could not help but feel that, in assessing the relative news value of father and son, the editorial department of the *Methodist Recorder* had very much fallen in line with modern attitudes. Television certainly has quite an impact.

After five years in television (which is noticeably less than forty years) David Frost had made himself one of the most discussed and written about personalities in Britain. He had considerably more power and influence than any other twenty-eight-year-old in the country, more than many an older man who regarded himself as a force in the land. Cabinet ministers, such as George

Brown and Denis Healey, Prime Ministers (Ian Smith), religious leaders (the Archbishop of Canterbury), kings (Hussein of Jordan), showed themselves willing, eager, to subject themselves to searching cross-examination in front of his audience, to discuss and/or justify their actions. Men such as Dr. Savundra and Dr. Petro were only too glad to go through a form of "trial by Television", with Frost as judge, prosecutor and jury.

Down from Cambridge with a B.A. degree ("Which I got on ability to waffle"), Frost burst forth upon the television public as linkman with *That Was The Week That Was* and, through this and similar programmes which followed, so forcibly took over the role of satirist-in-chief of the airwaves that his *Frost Over England* beat all comers from around the world in achieving the main accolade at the Montreux television festival. Having done that, he then turned to the more serious business of establishing himself as the most provocative, most influential of the television interviewers. He found himself in a position of being offered (and accepting) a fee of £500 per minute to do four shows for an American network. He became a producer (*At Last the 1948 Show*, among others). An impresario (David Paradine Productions). A business tycoon (leading light of the new London Weekend T.V. consortium). Best-selling author (*To England With Love*). As the parodist of *Time* magazine put it, "Where it will all end, knows God."

What manner of man is this who, still in his twenties, had already been able, in a mere five years, to carve out for himself a career on which a man twice his age might well feel proud to look back?

10

If you would understand the Frost syndrome you should have knowledge of three books – *What Makes Sammy Run?*, Dale Carnegie's *How to Win Friends and Influence People* and *The Man in the Grey Flannel Suit*. Therein is contained all one need know about what makes David Frost tick.

On the supposition that perhaps not everybody is familiar with each of these three books, it should be explained how they reflect the Frost personality.

The Sammy of *What Makes Sammy Run?* started as an office boy with a burning ambition to be a Big Operator, a young man always hustling to get ahead and, in spite of constantly being snubbed, despite all the rebuffs and the attempts to cut him down to size he eventually hit the Big Time in the entertainment world.

At Cambridge, Frost was a year behind the bright young men who were to become the nucleus of *Beyond the Fringe*, the Establishment Club and the whole start of the wave of satire that broke out at the beginning of the 1960s. So keen was he to become part of it all that it was said of him that "he was always yapping around their heels like a terrier". The comment has been made that "they were the Sixth Formers and they treated him like a Third Form fag". Taken on as a trainee by one of the big television companies, his pressing desire to get on to the T.V. screen was constantly rebuffed and as someone who was on the staff at the time has put it: "He was really just the fellow who got cigarettes and coffee for the boss."

But that boss now works for David Frost. The satirists of the early 1960s now work for David Frost when he chooses to hire them. "We all now work for David," says Elkan Allan. "He has done what everybody wants to do. He has made everybody eat humble pie — and at his table."

Dale Carnegie's *How to Win Friends*, first published in 1937, was a most frightening book which listed all the short-cuts to providing yourself with an 'ersatz' personality which would make you LIKED.

One cannot help but notice how, in private life, David Frost is liked by everyone who comes in contact with him – except those in the business who envy his success.

Two typical reactions to Frost off the T.V. screen : —

Lord Arran had this to say in one of his newspaper columns : "Having written rather rude things about Mr. David Frost, I found myself with him televising to Canada. We talked a little and once again I genuinely liked him. Whatever he may be like on television, in private life he shows beautiful manners towards older people – I am old enough to be his father — and that always endears me to young people."

Freddie Grisewood, reminiscing about his twenty years as chairman of the radio programme *Any Questions*, wrote : "When David Frost came on the programme, I didn't think I'd like him at first. He doesn't show the best side of himself on television but when he came on to the programme everyone fell for him. A charming man."

He is considerate. He has great concern for people. For example, once when Peter Ustinov was on his programme it was intended that he would have the first half, while the second would be devoted to a man with interesting views on graphology. The man had all his charts lined up ready and it was obviously going to be his big moment. But Frost got so wound up with Ustinov that he overran into the second half and in fact the end came with no time left for another guest. Immediately the programme was off the air Frost scurried in and out between the cameras and the monitors in search of the graphologist, to ease his disappointment with an apology and to stroll out of the studio with him. In like circumstances, other television stars are known to delegate this to the producer – or overlook it entirely.

Diana Crawfurd of Noel Gay Artists, his agents, has said: "David is the most courteous artist we have on our books. All the office boys and the secretaries on the staff like this. Most artists sail past office people, but never David. As a result people find themselves doing little things for him — like picking up his car for him from the north of Scotland."

He remembers people's names, which always makes them feel good. A girl who had a lowly job at Rediffusion when Frost started in television there, passed him in a hallway when he returned, five years later, to star in a programme for them. He was being escorted by a batch of Rediffusion top brass to their conference room and she was surprised and pleased when he called to her as he went by, "Hello, Sheila, how are you!"

At a party Frost overheard a girl telling a friend that she had achieved what every girl who makes the break from home wants – she had just acquired a flat of her very own. But unfortunately, by the time she had paid for the lease and other essentials, she had no money left to get a mattress for her bed. Next day a Harrods van made a delivery at her flat – a mattress, but with no indication as to who her benefactor was. Frost frequently does what James Barrie once described as "the best sort of kindness – kindness by stealth". The late Tony Hancock's former wife, Freddie Ross, who received much kindness from Frost during a difficult period of her life, says: "David is a very hard man to thank."

The impeccable manners mentioned by Lord Arran are not only towards older people. But an associate of Frost who is perhaps not as closely associated with him as he would like to be has said: "With Frost it is more than good manners. It is a studied way of behaviour. One can't always believe it is sincere. It's nice to have, of course. It's nice to hear people say you're losing weight even though you know darn well you aren't. It's strictly Dale Carnegie stuff. I don't know whether he's read *How to Win Friends* but he acts it to the life. If you want a manual of David Frost's behaviour, go to *How to Win Friends and Influence People*. It's all there."

If you *do* go to *How to Win Friends* you will find that the first Rule laid down by Dale Carnegie is: "Become genuinely interested in other people." Frost's concern about other people extends far beyond whether or not they are managing to lose weight. Rule Two is: "Smile." Frost smiles broadly and frequently not only on his programme but off. It could have been the prototype of the sort of smile Carnegie advises the would-be friend-winner to adopt – "a heart-warming smile, a smile that comes from within, the kind of smile that will bring a good price in the market-place." Rule Three: "Remember that a man's name is to him the sweetest and most important sound in the English language." Frost's uncanny ability to remember people's names never ceases

14

to astound, especially those briefly met and encountered some considerable time later. Rule Four: "Be a good listener." If Carnegie had wanted to illustrate this he could not have done better than run a photograph of the familiar sight of Frost at a party, head down, listening attentively, taking in every word somebody is saying to him.

One could go through the whole list of Rules in *How to Win Friends and Influence People* and give Frost a plus mark for each. One would be tempted to believe that he has studied and applied the Carnegie tenets so assiduously that he is a graduate with honours in this extended course on how to provide yourself with a synthetic personality. More than 6,000,000 people have bought copies of *How to Win Friends*. David Frost is not one of them.

But someone who has spent much time with Frost has said: "I cannot credit that it is all an act with him. It would be difficult – I would say impossible – to put on a front like that and keep it up all day, day after day, without slipping up every now and then, without an unguarded display of ill temper or lack of consideration for others that would give the game away. But if you seek to find such a chink in the Frost armour, you wait in vain. I am convinced it all stems from natural charm. He is such a basically nice person that people who feel they can be excused for doing dirt and riding rough-shod because they are caught up in the hurly-burly of television and similar rat races, secretly resent the fact that Frost doesn't indulge in such things. So they put it about that it is a contrived form of behaviour by Frost as part of his public relations."

The Man in the Grey Flannel Suit, filmed with Gregory Peck, has as its theme the basic conflict within themselves that many men have to face up to – the question: "Do I knock myself out becoming a big shot in my work, devoting all my time to furthering my ambition, or do I regard it just as a nine-to-five job and spend my spare time enjoying my family, my hobbies and other relaxations?"

The men who do become big operators do not debate in their minds at the outset which alternative they will choose. They have built-in Big Time drive and it never enters their heads to settle for being nine-to-fivers. David Frost is one such. Peter Cook recalls Frost's early dedication to being something more than just a performer. "At Cambridge, when Anglia T.V. did an excerpt from the Footlights show we just went through our routines as though we were on the stage, and the fact that the cameras were there was just incidental. But not David. He was all eyes for the cameras, conscious of them and the technique of how the television show was getting on the air, asking all sorts of questions of the studio people."

There are many today who would love to be in Frost's shoes. But it wouldn't do them any good, because the shoes wouldn't fit. They are just performers and will never be anything more. Frost always wanted to and has graduated from performer to impresario.

"Being David Frost requires a tremendous amount of work," a friend commented to Freddie Ross. "It's a twenty-four-hour job." To which Freddie Ross said: "David doesn't work twenty-four hours a day. He works twenty-eight. He borrows four from tomorrow."

16

The performers feel that they have to relax from the rat race and take time off for ego-building. After finishing what they feel is a good show they like to go to pub or club with "How'm-I-doing?" written all over them to pick up a batch of plaudits. Freddie Ross says: "David doesn't have time to enjoy his pinnacles." George Brightwell, his production manager, says: "It isn't a matter of his not enjoying his pinnacles. David gets his kicks out of going from one pinnacle straight on to the next. When he won the Montreux award I said to him, 'How about that, eh, David!' and he said, 'How about us getting back to work on those figures for the consortium for London weekends?' "

Chapter 2

The Young Frost

David Frost is a small town boy by birth and upbringing. He was in his twenties before he moved to the big city, where he has, as yet, spent very little of his life. He loves the small town atmosphere and its people. He feels they are the heart of England.

He was born, on 7 April 1939, in Tenterden, Kent, a town which now has a population of 5,370 and is so little known that if you phone Directory Enquiries the girl will ask you to "spell the name of the place you want". The guide books tell us that "Tenterden nestles in the Weald of Kent", but there is nothing much else it does. It has long been a popular place for retired people. An attractive enough town, with good shops, it is a veritable hot-bed of religion. Its churches outnumber its pubs – two Anglican, three Baptist, one Roman Catholic, a Methodist and a Unitarian, not to mention the Salvation Army. The local people are proud that David Frost comes from their home town but if any of them tell you they remember him from his days there they must have an extraordinary memory: he was transported from Tenterden when he was barely more than a year old.

The reason he was born there was that his father, the Rev. Wilfred Paradine Frost, was minister at one of the churches, the Oaks Road Methodist Church. The Frosts already had two daughters, Margaret, now married to a surveyor and estate agent in Whitby, and Jean, wife of a missionary doctor in Nigeria. When David was born, both of them were already in their teens and the age gap is such that he used to call himself P.S. David Frost. His father was thrilled to have a son. In Tenterden's high street someone met the doctor who had delivered the late arrival and asked how the Rev. Frost felt about it. "He has wings," said the doctor.

Frost says that the Paradine of his father's name, which is also his own middle name, stems from the Paradines who came to England from the Netherlands in 1497 or 1597, he is not quite sure which. He is also uncertain about the pronunciation, varying in conversation between Paradyne and Paradeen. He says he is the last in line to perpetuate the name and to make sure that it doesn't die he has called his television producing company David Paradine Productions. However, the London telephone directory tells us that a Mr. A. J. Paradine of Edgware (no relation) is also helping him to keep the name alive.

Frost's father was accepted into the Methodist ministry in 1927. The Methodist church is an itinerant ministry, though not as itinerant as it used to be. Originally, Methodist ministers would spend only a couple of years in one place before moving on. Now the stay is usually from five to seven years. In his forty years of service to the church the Rev. Frost got through Horsham (Sussex), Burnley (Lancashire), Tenterden (Kent), Kempston (Bedfordshire), Gillingham (Kent), Raunds (Northamptonshire) and Beccles (Suffolk). Wherever he went the size of the congregations grew and new church

19

buildings sprang up. In Gillingham, on the Eastcourt Estate, a completely new church stands as a monument to his efforts. Apart from Gillingham, which was a veritable metropolis of 68,000 when he lived there, David Frost's youth was spent in little communities of 4,000 to 8,000.

Having been born in the year World War II broke out, Frost has vivid memories of the first time he saw those things which war-time rations and restrictions denied him. Many such people recall eating their first orange or banana or other exotic food, which virtually disappeared from the tables of war-time Britons. But Frost's most vivid memory was of something different. "I remember the thrill I got when I saw my first lead pencil with a coloured exterior. I don't mean a coloured pencil, I mean an ordinary lead pencil painted blue, say, or yellow or red. All the pencils I had ever known had been just plain wood, but a shiny painted one – what luxury! I suppose I was about six at the time. Then when they were allowed to make pencils with rubbers on the end again, that was beyond my wildest dreams. And another milestone I remember was when they took sweets off the ration, just after the war – and had to put them back on the ration again, quick, because we went berserk."

Although it would not be accurate to say that Frost grew up in a poor home, the fact remains that when the Rev. Frost died in 1967 his stipend had risen only to the current rate for Methodist ministers – £500 to £600 a year. At Methodist headquarters in London they will tell you that "this is not hardship and not opulence". But around £10 a week would seem to be a little bit meagre for a minister's family to live on with the cost of living the way it is. Granted a manse and certain "ministerial allowances" go with the stipend but Mrs. Frost, who of course had even less to work with back in the days when bringing up her children, must have made great calls on her ingenuity and self denial.

Today Frost says: "The thing I will always wonder about is how my mother and father managed to make life at home so comfortable – in addition to being so warm and all those things for which I owe so much to them. And the food so good and so on. It's just magic how they did it."

"Your father had no other income?"

"No, he didn't. And it's not just the fact that the salary is so small but with it goes the place of a leader of the community and Methodist ministers are not encouraged to go around in overalls."

"A B.B.C. handout says that you were offered a Public School education and turned it down."

"That's right."

"But surely it would have been difficult for your father to finance it."

"I think he was thinking in terms of the scholarships that some boarding schools offer for ministers' sons."

"Why did you turn it down?"

"Life was far too interesting at home."

"Do you ever regret not having been to Public School?"

"No, never. I personally don't think that a boarding school education is needed – except when, for instance, the parents are abroad, or special care is needed, or the parents are divorced.

"I am not a passionate opponent of the Public Schools. I don't consider them a terrible vice. I just consider they are an example of a wrong priority, in the sense that any specially good facilities and any special amounts of care shouldn't be lavished just on people who can afford to pay, or would probably get by anyway – but on those who really need the education. So I think – not because the Public Schools are odious or anything like that – I think it would be an extremely good move if the Public Schools were changed overnight to schools for the less naturally academic children or the educationally sub-normal. Now that, obviously, in basic terms is not practical, and it's not a class move, but it would just seem to me to be a more worthwhile priority."

Frost started his schooling at a Froebel school in Bedford. Frederich Froebel, as anyone who looks him up in an encyclopedia knows, was one of the first to use the free-expression approach to children in kindergarten. But this Froebel freedom which young David enjoyed until he was eight led to a misunderstanding when his family moved from Bedfordshire to Gillingham and he entered his first conventional council school. It was the Barnsole Road Boys' Primary and Frost came under Mrs. May Goodwin. Now retired, she was one of those dedicated teachers who appear to have total recall in respect of some, if not all of their pupils.

"The day David made his first appearance at our school stands out in my memory," she says. "It was September 1947. I had almost finished marking my register when the headmaster walked in with a plump, fresh faced, well groomed, intelligent looking boy, who

22

appeared to be very self-possessed. 'A new boy for you, Mrs. Goodwin,' he said. 'Oh, no,' I replied. 'That makes forty-eight.' 'Sorry, Mrs. Goodwin, I cannot put him anywhere else.' As if to mollify me, he added: 'He seems to be a very intelligent boy and –' with a pause '– he is also a parson's son.' The headmaster gave me his particulars, such as date of birth and name. 'David –' a pause '– Paradine Frost.' 'You mean Paradise Lost?' I came back with. He smiled and David was often referred to by the staff as 'Paradise Lost'.

"I said, 'Sit down, Frost,' directing him to a front seat. For many days to follow I was continually saying 'Sit down, Frost,' because he was for ever coming out of his seat to ask me questions. It was clear David had to learn discipline. I began to think he was a precocious child, always wanting to be in the limelight.

"Then, by chance, at half term I learned what he was really like. I was having coffee one day when someone I knew came in and surprised me by saying, 'How is David Frost getting on?' I asked her what she knew about him and she said that her father and the Rev. Frost were great friends. I told her my impressions. When she said 'Well, he loves you,' I was flabbergasted. I thought he must be heartily sick of me saying 'Sit down, Frost.' Then she told me something of his background. It completely changed my attitude towards him. David wanted organised tuition. He was eager to learn. But he had never been in a primary school before, only a Froebel, where class discipline is unknown and a child learns only if he wants to. There the classes are very much smaller, and naturally one could give individual attention. David had been used to this.

"David integrated into the class very quickly and soon had lots of friends. He loved football and followed Gillingham's career ardently and most other teams too, learning the names of all the players, which he seemed to have an uncanny knack of remembering. This fact alone gained him friends. He had a *very* friendly nature, never at a loss for words in a conversation and a very good vocabulary. He wound up second in the class and would have been first but lost marks for bad writing – which is even worse today!

"I could not say that he was an outstanding boy, but as the scholarship class master said, 'He was a boy of good average ability'."

Despite Mrs. Goodwin's crack about "Paradise Lost", it did not really catch on as a nickname. At school Frost was known as "Jack" – "It's something everybody who is named Frost has to put up with!" he says. "Like 'Dusty' Rhodes – everyone must call you 'Jack' Frost."

He bears out what his old teacher says of his love of soccer. "I was one of those kids who lived to put coats down and bang a ball about. I think the only thing that persuaded me to learn to read was so that I could study the football results." For the town of Gillingham it was a big event when their football team was re-elected to the Football League in 1950. Young David was taken along regularly to see Gillingham in action by his father, who was admitted free, team officials being of the opinion that it raised the tone of the proceedings to have a man of the cloth on the touchline each week. One of Frost's best remembered birthday presents was the one he got on his eleventh birthday – a season ticket for Gillingham, which made him a hit among the new boys when he enrolled at his next school.

At Gillingham Grammar School they are proud and pleased to be able to number David Frost among their old boys. One might even say that they are overjoyed, because when they were asked the names of other pupils who had become famous they replied: "Professor Tress, Professor of Economics at Bristol University, and Mr. John Boulter, principal singer of the Black and White Minstrels." Which, to say the least, is a rather slim output in the field of illustrious Old Boys.

Frost was one of six hundred boys at the school from 1950 to 1954 and John Hicks, headmaster, recalls: "He had considerable intellectual ability, particularly in science, where his work was of real promise. He was a leader of his contemporaries with a lively mind, a pleasant and polite manner, and a keen sense of humour. He was not interested in rugby, which is our main winter game, and had to satisfy his enthusiasm for soccer outside the school. He was good at cricket."

Frost has paid only one return visit to the school, in 1964 when at the height of his *That Was The Week* fame. The headmaster had invited him to open the school fête. It was indeed a coup when he accepted. Frost flew from America to keep the engagement and the headmaster remembers: "On this occasion he created a very good impression indeed, not only giving generously of his time and money to help the School, but showing a genuine interest in it. At his own request during this visit he met once again all those masters still on the staff who had taught him and shared reminiscences with them.

25

"I was struck by his wit and his excellent sense of timing which contributed so much to the entertaining speech he made and also, in his private conversations, by his essential humility, a quality which is not obvious from his television appearances."

In 1954 the Frosts moved from Gillingham to Raunds, Northamptonshire, where the Rev. Frost took over the Brook Street Church.

Raunds, which has a population nudging 5,000 and a cluster of boot and shoe factories, is not a particularly attractive town. Even the Official Handbook admits that "the domestic architecture is, alas, not of very high quality". Grown up from a settlement started by Saxon colonists around A.D. 700, it has short, interwoven streets with unusual names, like Toothill ("toot" being Anglo-Saxon for "look-out"). A narrow road which turns off from the end of the main street has the odd name of Titty Ho, of which the handbook says "no probable meaning has yet been discovered". It is the Lovers' Lane of Raunds.

But the cliff on the edge of which part of the town is built ("raunds": Anglo-Saxon for "edge") gives it a certain character. As the handbook says: "Even a factory (Tebbutt & Hall, Boots and Shoes) can look impressive when perched on the side of a precipice. The neighbouring Methodist church would not appear half so grand were it not on an eminence above the street."

Methodism is strong in Raunds since, besides the Anglican Parish Church, Methodists are the only others catered for in the town. So the Rev. Frost was an important member of the community, and David joined

26

his father and mother in playing an active part in the religious and community life.

Although still only in his teens, David went into the pulpit as a lay preacher. As he warmed to his work, he was soon starting to pull in the crowds. "It was his asides that did it," says Mrs. Frost. "The congregation *does* have a tendency to go to sleep and David used to wake them up with a smile."

This foretaste of the Frost technique in television was accompanied by much activity in putting on shows in the Brook Street Hall, productions in which he was at once producer, stage manager, script-writer and star.

Mr. Wesley Lawrence owned a sports boots factory in Raunds (David got his soccer boots wholesale) and his wife, Gladys Lawrence tells of the Frost boy being a frequent visitor at their home. For one thing, they had a television set, which was a lack at the Methodist manse – "Good play on tonight, Mrs. Lawrence. Mind if I watch?" But the Lawrences had something else which was even more of a magnet to David. At that time when such things were not as common as they are today the Lawrences had, wonder of wonders, a tape recorder! Many an hour was spent in listening to his voice bringing to perfection imitations of Eamonn Andrews doing *This Is Your Life*, Gilbert Harding on *What's My Line?* and other shows which loomed large in television at that period, and polishing up material he would use in what he called his "Spotlight Concerts" at the Methodist Hall.

It was some years before he was able to afford a tape recorder of his own. During his life in Raunds, money was not plentiful. One Christmas, to augment his pocket money, he did the postal rounds. "I remember the chief postmaster was named George Cheese. He used to come in from the sorting room and say things like, 'I see the Perkins are away in Spain. They're having a very good time, but they've had rain.' He used to have a good squint at all the postcards. I remember one day he came in absolutely affronted. 'Look at this! Look at this!' he said. Someone had sent a card home that started, 'Dear Mum, Dad and Mr. Cheese.'"

Frost's schooling when he was at Raunds could have taken a different course. When the family arrived there arrangements were made for him to get a grant from the Northamptonshire education authority to go to Kimbolton, a Public School not far from the town. But his mother recalls that he was quite firm about turning the idea down. " 'I'm not going there,' he said. 'I'd be better educated at a grammar school.' So plans were changed and he went to Wellingborough Grammar School, about eight miles from Raunds."

At Wellingborough, Headmaster H. A. Wrenn's main remembrance of the "cheerful, well liked" David was that he was "one of the best actors we ever had". And as well as being a leading light in the school's drama competitions, he also got in some early practice in the field of public speaking in such things as the Public Reading Competition.

He was a star of the school cricket team but his love of soccer created a problem for him. Wellingborough Grammar is not only a rugby school but ardently rugger. They are proud of the International players they have produced. These include Don White, the forward who was fourteen times capped for England, and John Hyde,

28

who had that rare distinction of being capped while still a schoolboy. Jeff Butterfield, acknowledged one of the world's best centres in postwar rugby, was physical exercise master at Wellingborough when Frost was there. Frost used to have a tussle with his conscience as far as rugby was concerned. He played soccer each Saturday for the Raunds Town soccer team in the United Counties League. At school he had loyalty to his House and always wanted to play well enough for them at rugger to help them win their house matches, but not so well that he would find himself being picked for the School XV and thus deny himself his beloved soccer on Saturdays. He managed to pull it off all right and was on duty each week with his soccer pals at Berrister Field at Raunds, while the Wellingborough XV were chasing around after the other shaped ball.

He was not only mad about soccer but also very good at it. He might well have been making headlines on the sports pages today. A talent scout for Nottingham Forest was very taken with him and the club tried to sign him up. But in those days (the late 1950s) professional soccer players had not yet been released from their serfdom; anyone entering the sport could see no vistas of earning big money. Compared with the possibilities in the youthful Frost's other love, television, the financial outlook was bleak. Faced with the choice of being a soccer star such as Stanley Matthews at £20 a week or a television star like Gilbert Harding at £300, Frost didn't take long to make his mind up. He turned down the £12 a week which Notts Forest offered him.

In between all this extra-curricular activity at Wellingborough Grammar, he did manage to get some school work done and won what used to be known as a State Scholarship to Cambridge.

While waiting to get a place at the university, he spent a year as a teacher at Irthlingborough County primary school, some four miles from his home in Raunds. Mr. W. E. Lawrence, headmaster at the school, recalls that Frost "had a wonderful knack with boys. He would have made a first-rate schoolmaster." When the schools' inspector paid his call at Irthlingborough that year he talked to the young teacher whom the headmaster highly commended. "How do you see your future?" the inspector asked. "I have my sights on television," said the nineteen-year-old Frost.

"I found my year of teaching at Irthlingborough a very exciting time," says Frost. "If I wasn't involved in all this television that's what I'd do, teach, particularly in a secondary modern school. I remember I was in charge of all the History but the official syllabus tended to stop short, so that, if children left after the first term of their fourth year – when they got to fifteen – they would have got up to about 1700! I switched it to 20th century history, in the hope that it might at least have some relevance to the lives they were going to lead.

"There is the danger that children will leave school knowing how to multiply 17 over 112 by 43 over 2, but nothing about how they are going to live, nothing about how to sort out facts from opinions."

His years from 1958 to 1961 at Gonville and Caius College, Cambridge, where he read English, followed the pattern he had set at Wellingborough – heavy concentration on the fringe aspects such as Drama Society etc. and just enough attention to the tuition side to get his degree. "I didn't do any work really. I took purple hearts and didn't go to bed for the five nights of the Tripos exam." Tutors at Cambridge feel themselves bound by the same code of ethics as doctors and lawyers – they will not discuss their clients. But one of them told a friend recently: "I found Frost had a mind like a vacuum cleaner – pick up anything. And highly developed verbal dexterity."

When he had his eyes set on Cambridge originally his parents had told him that he would have to do it on his own, since they certainly couldn't afford it. He said: "I'll get to Cambridge. I'd like to run the Foot-lights. And I'd like to edit *Granta*." He achieved all three.

There was some surprise at Cambridge when he was chosen editor of *Granta*, that sporadic periodical which has a very up-and-down existence, both editorially and financially, depending on just how good each editor is. It seems that Frost got the editorial chair because his predecessor, Willie Dunlop, wanted to be regarded as a great *Granta* editor in retrospect and what better way to do it than elect as successor someone who would not shine? Frost, however, upset this plan by doing rather a good job as editor. It made money when he was at the helm – which could not be said for *his* successor. When Frost became a T.V. star one of his first fund-raising activities was the staging of a show to help raise the £3,000 needed to save *Granta* from extinction.

His Footlights exploits are gone into more fully later in this book. It was the repercussions of what he did in this annual revue at the Arts Theatre in Cambridge in May Week, rather than the show itself, which were to have such a bearing on his future – a future that was to benefit greatly from his having been to Cambridge.

Going to Cambridge saved Frost. For one thing, apart from rounding him out as a thinking person, it fixed up his accent. It put a veneer on the Grammar school voice, not taking it up into the undesirable lah-dee-dah, but eliminating the more unattractive elements of a speaking voice which those who hire and fire find a shortcoming. Frost emerged from Cambridge with a good classless voice, ideal for television talk pro-grammes. No one can feel superior about it; it makes no listener feel inferior.

A conference discussion for a Frost show. The names were written in by Frost himself.

With Paul Getty and Cliff Michelmore.

Chapter 3

The Breakthrough

When David Frost came down from Cambridge in 1961, with his mother's frying pan, to set up house in Park Crescent Mews, Victoria, and to make the big assault on London, cash was very short indeed. On weekends, when he would visit his father and mother in Beccles he could not afford the train fare and used to hitch-hike the 109 miles back to London.

"We used to drive him to Blythburgh," Mrs. Frost recalls. "It is on the main Lowestoft-to-London road and on Sunday evenings there is always lots of traffic going back to town. We used to leave him by the side of the road, drive on a little way and then stop to look back to see that he got a lift all right. Whenever my husband and I passed the spot we always used to think back to those days. The other day I happened to drive past with one of my grandchildren in the car and I told him about how we used to leave David there. He said: 'Just fancy! Uncle David having to hitch-hike!'"

Fresh from university, Frost had two promising channels to explore in the entertainment world – cabaret and television.

It was the Denmark Street agency, Noel Gay Artists, which opened up the vistas for him as a nightclub entertainer. As part of their talent spotting they always see to it that someone in the firm has a look at each year's Footlights show at Cambridge. Richard Armitage, a director of the agency, recalls now that when he saw young Frost in action in the 1961 show he thought his material was not all that good. "But he had the characteristic of bringing his own atmosphere with him on to the stage. After his first appearance I couldn't take much interest in other things in the show, waiting for him to come back on again." He signed up Frost and his perspicacity has paid big dividends for Noel Gay Artists, since throughout Frost's ever expanding success saga they have remained his sole agents.

Frost started off on his nightclub career at the Blue Angel, in Mayfair. Originally made for one week, the engagement was extended to two months, although the fee was not high by nightclub standards. Of course, he was to have the satisfaction of returning to the Blue Angel, at three times the original fee and with great success, when he was at the height of his *That Was The Week That Was* fame. The thing *could* have come around full circle with Frost winding up by owning the place. When Max Setty died, the Blue Angel went into a decline and in 1967 Frost was one of those who started negotiations to buy it. But it was left to somebody else to take over and put the club back on its feet, Frost withdrawing when he realised that to run the place properly would have called on too much of his personal time.

Concurrent with his first excursion into cabaret, Frost had embarked on his television career.

Rediffusion had a scheme whereby they picked each year what they felt were the two most promising university graduates to be trained by them for a television

34

career. In 1961 when David Frost came before Rediffu-sion's selection board they were unanimous that he was by far the brightest of all the young hopefuls they had interviewed. But there were reservations about taking him on. As one member of the board put it: "Don't you think he's a bit *too* bright? Don't you think he'll prove a nuisance to us?" But Elkan Allan, at that time pro-ducer of the current affairs programme *This Week*, was enthusiastic about the possibilities of the young Frost. He said "I'll take him in *This Week* – whatever. Heaven knows we're short enough of bright people".

So the twenty-two-year-old Frost came on to the staff of *This Week* and embarked on his training in the techni-calities and techniques of television. But not many months had gone by before he started to become frus-trated at not being able to get on to the screen. Elkan Allan had been moved from *This Week* to be Head of Entertainment Programmes and Cyril Bennett was his successor as producer of the programme. But despite Frost's persistence in trying to get before the cameras, Bennett would not have him on the screen at any price. He felt that Frost looked all wrong for television. What-ever his talents he was "totally unsuitable" to appear on the box. The nearest Frost got to getting on the screen for *This Week* was to be allowed to be the voice off-camera asking questions when they went out doing street interviews.

The book world has its publishers who will tell you of their sad claim to fame, that they turned down *Room At the Top* or *Born Free* or some other best seller which was not at once embraced in manuscript form. Cyril Bennett is the equivalent in the television world. "I was the man who wouldn't put Frost on the screen," he says now with a wry smile. But the ending has proved to be a happy one. Cyril Bennett now works with Frost. When executive appointments were being made for the new London Weekend Television, Bennett was given the plum job of Controller of Programmes.

But to return to Frost, the television trainee at Rediffusion . . . Elkan Allan did not share the view of Cyril Bennett and others at *This Week* that Frost should merely be heard and not seen on T.V.. As soon as he could he arranged to have him transferred to Entertainment and in June, 1961, Frost made his first appearance on the major television networks. He was compère of three programmes devoted to the Twist. The first was a competition to find the best Twister in England, then it was *Let's Twist* in Paris and finally on the Riviera. Such was the impact of the young man "totally unsuitable" to be seen on the T.V. screen that even today those Twist programmes stay in the mind of those who happened to see them. Elkan Allan was amazed at the inborn television expertise of this young man down from Cambridge who had never before tackled the complicated and harassing job of handling outside broadcasts of this nature. What especially impressed Allan was that the Riviera programme was designed as a gay, sunny, bikini-clad romp but was in fact done in a downpour of rain. Frost carried it all off as though such television disasters were something he had been coping with for years.

At that time something new had hit the entertainment world and it had been given the catch-all term of "satire". *Beyond the Fringe* at the Fortune Theatre had started it all. The Establishment Club was its extension. Television felt that it really must hop on the satire bandwagon, and at the B.B.C. Ned Sherrin, at the instigation of Donald Baverstock, was getting together a late night show called *That Was The Week That Was*.

One evening at a party someone came up to Allan and said that he had seen a dry run of *That Was The Week*. Allan naturally embraced this opportunity to learn something of the opposition's plan and was all questions. His informant saved the clincher for the end.

"Do you know who their linkman is?" he said to Allan.

"No."

"Your boy, David Frost."

First thing next morning Allan taxed Frost with this and he admitted it was true.

"Perhaps I shouldn't have done it, but I did," said Frost.

"Why didn't you ask me whether you could do it?"

"I thought you wouldn't let me."

"I certainly wouldn't have let you."

Allan told him that he had no option but to report the matter to John McMillan, Rediffusion's Controller of Programmes.

On the carpet before the Controller, Frost received a lecture on loyalty from McMillan.

Elkan Allan interceded on Frost's behalf, suggesting that if the B.B.C. wanted him for *their* show, Rediffusion should make a counter offer to retain him and make him linkman for *What the Public Wants*, their satire show to compete with that of the B.B.C.. Frost relates that he was offered a four-year contract to stay, which on the face of it appeared a much better deal than a contract for thirteen weeks of preparing *TW3* for the B.B.C., and an option for a further thirteen weeks if it went on the air. After four or five days of hectic conferring, Frost decided to take the gamble and go to the B.B.C..

John McMillan was doubly enraged about the Frost affair. In the first place he felt it a breach of ethics for someone to accept the training facilities of an organisation and then go across the road to give the opposition the benefit. And secondly Frost, as everybody knows, was a spectacular success as linkman for *TW3*. Had he flopped, McMillan would have had some sort of solace. But as *TW3* grew more and more popular, and Rediffusion's *What the Public Wants* came and went, unpraised and soon forgotten, the deeper became the wound. A measure of how much it rankled with McMillan was to be seen in the fact that when Elkan Allan took David Frost to lunch to see whether he could woo him back to Rediffusion, Allan's expense chit was not okayed. Allan was told he had no right to take to lunch somebody whom Rediffusion wanted to have nothing whatsoever to do with. "I will not even have his name mentioned in this building," said McMillan.

Before passing on to the intriguing story of how it was sheer luck that *That Was The Week* and linkman Frost got on the air at all, one should perhaps look back objectively on that little contretemps at Rediffusion. Just how "unethical" Frost had been was open to question. If what he had done *was* unethical, then there are a lot of people being unethical in all spheres of business, day after day. If it is a bad thing that a lowly paid employee who is not given full opportunity to prove his worth manages to better himself across the road, then highly paid executives who dally with the opposition on the quiet and then make the switch must be very bad indeed.

Frost's breakthrough with *That Was The Week That Was* was a perfect illustration of the old saying that it is all very well to have talent but you also have to have the luck to go with it.

It was through not one but two strokes of good fortune that Frost was able to make *TW3* the launching pad for his ascent into the higher realms of television. In the first place, he was lucky to get the try-out as linkman for the programme, since he was by no means first choice for the job. And the second piece of luck was that the pilot programme of *TW3* was rejected by the B.B.C. planners, the whole thing was shelved and it was only by the purest chance, an odd turn of events, that it became a television series.

It was in the early summer of 1962 that Ned Sherrin followed up Baverstock's idea of a T.V. show that would cash in on the satire vogue and, when casting the pilot version, which he hoped would convince his superiors it should be put on, it was natural that he should turn to the satire experts – the *Beyond the Fringe* quartet and the performers at the *Fringe* offshoot, the Establishment Club. He approached Peter Cook to be linkman of his project. But Cook was too busy, what with appearing in *Beyond the Fringe* and being the leading light of the Establishment. The stage show was going to the States, anyway, so he would not have been

able to carry through with the television series if the
B.B.C. decided to embrace it. So Sherrin had to try someone else. He chose John Bird, star performer at the
Establishment. Bird accepted and the plans got under
way for Sherrin's show with Bird in the chair. It was
decided he should have a side-kick and Sherrin looked
around for a likely prospect for this job.

At that time Sherrin, along with the multitude, did
not know of the existence of a young man called David
Frost. The first time he saw his name was in a copy of
Stage which, in the course of a review of the cabaret at
the Blue Angel, mentioned his act in friendly terms. The
story goes that Sherrin looked in at the Blue Angel that
night, only to learn that Frost had been dropped. The
management, he was told, were not sufficiently enthusiastic about his talents to make him a regular performer.
However, they were talked into re-instating him that
night so that Sherrin could size him up. And when he
saw him in action, Sherrin felt he had enough possibilities to be given a try as support to John Bird.

But today Frost says that this is a private joke between Sherrin and himself. "I always tell Ned that it is
a complete fabrication he has invented. I remember that
night and there was never any doubt about whether I
was going on or not. Max Setty didn't throw his money
about like that. But I suppose if the story gets repeated
enough, I will have to accept that history has been re-
written!"

At all events, during the making of the pilot of *TW3*,
John Bird cried off. Arrangements had been made to
start an Establishment Club in New York and the firm
offer of heading up the cast over there appealed more to

Bird than the nebulous prospect of the B.B.C. bosses giving *TW3* the go-ahead. Frost inherited his job.

That was lucky break number one for Frost. But he needed another before he was to make his impact on the little screen.

The pilot show was taped and it turned out to be something of a marathon – two and a half hours in all.

On a sweltering mid-summer afternoon Sherrin showed his brainchild to the assembled B.B.C. decision-makers, which was not the happiest of situations since he was asking them to simulate the mood of audiences watching a late-night show in mid-winter. They approached it with curiosity. Those who had seen advance snippets of some of the sketches had the look of men slipping in to see a blue movie.

Thumbs down was the decision. Nice try and all that, but too far out for the B.B.C. audience. *That Was The Week That Was* was put back in the can and that, apparently, was the end of that. Just one of numerous well intentioned ideas which never see the light of day.

However . . .

One item in the show had Bernard Levin delivering a little discourse to twenty-two ladies of the Conservative Party and acting as Aunt Sally to their questions. Two good laughs emerged from this sequence. One came when one of the Tory ladies said: "How would you like to have a daughter of yours out alone in a dark lane and nothing done about it?" The other was when one of the good ladies said not once but several times: "Mr. Macmillan has always satisfied me."

News reached the Conservative Central Office that there were great old chuckles going on within the B.B.C.

over some rather embarrassing things said inadvertently by some Tory ladies on a programme which, it was understood, was shortly to be broadcast. A strong complaint was made to Kenneth Adam, Director of Television at the B.B.C.. Not unnaturally, a complaint of this nature was one which had to be fully investigated. Kenneth Adam had not seen the *TW3* pilot. It was run through for him.

Great stuff! We'll start this programme in the autumn.

The achievement of *That Was The Week* was that it made its own peak viewing period at a time regarded in television circles as "dead". On Saturday nights at ten-thirty too many people are at pubs and parties for television to command a big audience. That was a proven fact in pre-*TW3* days. The late Saturday evening spot was lucky if it could attract 3,000,000 viewers. For comparison: 20,000,000 watching *Coronation Street*, early evening, mid-week. But in no time *TW3* had boosted the 3,000,000 to 11,000,000. It emptied the pubs. At parties when ten-thirty came round it was "Quiet, everybody, we're turning on *That Was The Week*". At offices on Monday mornings it was "Did you see that thing they did on *That Was The Week*!" and nobody could really get down to work until the programme's latest outrages had been thoroughly re-hashed.

"Seriously, though, you're doing a grand job," became the catchphrase of the day. Frost was asked how it had originated. "It wasn't planted in the programme as a catchphrase. It was just an ad-lib I did that caught on. It came from a Roy Kinnear monologue. Roy did an old style music hall comedian trying to entertain the troops and using the catchphrase, 'Seriously though, lads, you're doing a grand job'. Later in the show I had an item about something a bit ludicrous a fox-hunting chappie had said. I felt, as I read it, that the irony wasn't getting through to the audience, so at the end I added 'Seriously though, Mr. So-and-So, you're doing a grand job.' It got a big laugh. So I used it again on other programmes. But oddly enough, even though it became a vast catchphrase, it wasn't used on *TW3* more than six times. It was the public that took it over."

Everyone knew that David Frost was a Methodist minister's son and they wondered how his father and mother reacted to such things as the *Reader's Digest* take-off: "The Condensed Bible . . . Including: 'I've Heard of Natural Childbirth but This is Ridiculous' . . . 'Your Child May be More Gifted Than You Think (The Story of Mary and Joseph)' . . . 'The Resurrection: You Can't Keep a Good Man Down' . . ." It was pretty raw stuff for a parson to hear his son putting over on the box.

Looking back on the furore such items created in the country in general, and more particularly in the little community of Beccles, Suffolk, where the Rev. Frost and his wife were leaders of the Methodist Church, Mrs. Frost says now: "Some people in the Church complained to us about what David was doing. We got all sorts of phone calls and letters. We disliked some of the sketches. We felt David was cut out for better things. But he was of age and we felt that he must do what he wanted to do."

A neighbour who used to watch the show with the Frosts recalled that whenever a particularly racy item cropped up Mrs. Frost used to say: "Blue pencil, David, blue pencil!"

Letters poured into thè B.B.C. about *TW3*. Those which did not praise the show fell into two main categories. The first consisted of letters in which "disgusting" was the operative word. The other group were from young men requesting photographs of Frost so that they could get their barbers to copy his hairstyle, perhaps best described as a roll-top fringe and long since discarded by its originator.

Frost soon found himself receiving five hundred fan letters a week, which he asked the Correspondence department of the B.B.C. to handle for him, and which they promptly returned to him with the information that they provided such a service for performers on their staff but not for outsiders merely on contract. So Frost, at twenty-three, achieved what to most young men of ambition is the first real indication of the fact that one is going places – he hired his own private secretary. His advertisement stated that applicants must have "experience, efficiency and beauty". He said at the time that that was reasonable enough, since if one had to do a lot of dictating to someone, she might as well be attractive.

News could not help but reach America that there was a new, "different" sort of T.V. series that was creating a great stir in Britain and in due course it was decided to put out an American edition, with Frost the sole British ingredient. In that land of sponsored television, however, it had to be a much watered down version. What sponsor would, for instance, have risked the huge drop in sales of his product by allowing someone on his programme to say: "The rule in Roman Catholicism is DON'T – but if you must, confess as soon as possible afterwards."

Britishers who visited the States and saw the American version, found it a pale imitation of the original. But Frost came through fine.

There was no question that David Frost, new aspirant for the epithet of "T.V. personality", was MADE.

But there were at least four people who were not happy about David Frost becoming a success – the *Beyond the Fringe* quartet of Peter Cook, Dudley Moore, Jonathan Miller and Alan Bennett.

It is interesting to note now that it was generally believed that *Beyond the Fringe* was a show that four young men at Cambridge had been doing and it was brought into town by an enterprising management. That was not the case. The show had its roots in Edinburgh. In 1960 John Bassett was Assistant Artistic Director of the Edinburgh Festival and he suggested to Peter Cook that a little group be got together to stage an hour-long entertainment as part of the lighter side of that annual congress of the arts. Cook had just left Cambridge and was enjoying some success, if not public recognition, as a writer of revue material for such shows as Kenneth Williams' *Pieces of Eight* and *One Over the Eight*. His agent told Cook not to touch the Edinburgh idea, since it would be "damaging to his career". Fortunately for Cook, he ignored this sound advice and recruited Dudley Moore and Alan Bennett who had been at Oxford, and also Jonathan Miller, who had come down from Cambridge some years before and "had to be talked out of being a doctor". *Beyond the Fringe* was the hit of that

45

year's Edinburgh Festival and an instant success when it was brought to London in expanded form a couple of months later.

Beyond the Fringe ran for two years with the original cast at the Fortune Theatre and continued, with substitutes, when Cook and the other three went over to be just as big a hit on Broadway. And it was while they were in the States that Frost hit the headlines back home. They were quoted as being "furious" that Frost was apparently stealing their stuff for the larger television audience. "We created the conditions on which he is now thriving. *That Was The Week That Was* has cheapened it all."

However, Peter Cook will tell you now that their annoyance at that time was based on rather misleading reports from England. They had only fragmentary details of all the things Frost was supposed to be borrowing from them in their absence and in due course they were to find that it had all been rather exaggerated, especially by those who wished to stir up ill feeling between the originators of the satire craze and the newcomer. How short-lived was their period of being furious with Frost is shown by the fact that when he in turn followed them to the States to do *That Was The Week* for American viewers they invited him to stay with them at the summer house they had rented in Connecticut. And it was there that the swimming-pool incident occurred.

It is not widely known that Peter Cook saved Frost's life. One hot afternoon, when the Fringe crowd and Frost were relaxing at the pool behind the house, Cook was taking in the sun in a deck chair and was just dozing off when he heard a shout from Frost. He looked over, to see him in the deep end of the pool doing a wonderful take-off of somebody drowning. Or at least that was what Cook thought he was doing, until it became so realistic that Cook realised that he was in fact in difficulties. Cook dived in and fished Frost out. He was in none too good shape and had Cook not been so quick off the mark the consequences could have been serious.

Remembering it now, Cook says: "Thank God I did save him. With all that bad publicity at the time, if I hadn't saved him who wouldn't have believed that I'd pushed him in!"

In 1964 Ned Sherrin, who was eventually to leave television for movie-making with Columbia, fathered a successor to *That Was The Week*, and naturally Frost was in the chair. *Not So Much a Programme More a Way of Life* had a catchy signature tune, and it differed from *TW3* in that it was much more of a talk programme. The sketches were still there, the best of them superbly done by John Bird and Eleanor Bron, but the accent was more on discussion. Frost would usually have four guests, of whom Patrick Campbell, a newcomer to television, became very much a regular attraction. Sherrin announced that Frost's function was to "midwife the talk" and he fitted so happily into that niche that it really set the pattern for the Frost programmes as we know them today.

At this time he also set the pattern for his London-New York commuting which has earned him the title of "B.O.A.C.'s best trans-Atlantic customer". *Not So Much a Programme* ran through the 1964–5 winter

47

three nights a week, Friday–Saturday–Sunday, and at the same time Frost was doing his second series of the American version of *TW3*. His routine of flying to New York each Monday to do one show and flying back to London on Wednesday to prepare the other went on without let-up for six months – more than fifty Atlantic flights in twenty-six weeks. A Fleet Street sub-editor, in a flash of brilliance, dubbed a story about this: "A Male of Two Cities". Frost commented at the time: "Although I don't want to go on doing this all my life, for the moment it's great."

In point of fact he shows every sign of doing it all his life, since his trans-Atlantic trips have, if anything, increased in frequency in recent years. It is a commonplace now for anyone phoning Frost in London to hear his secretary say. "He went off to New York this morning. He'll be back tomorrow."

Chapter 4

Frost on High Ground

David Frost put the seal on his reputation as the public's most talked-about television personality and the hottest property in the T.V. business with two shows which hit their peak in 1967 – *The Frost Report* for the B.B.C. and *The Frost Programme* for Rediffusion.

They will tell you at the B.B.C.: "David Frost would not be where he is today but for two men – Ned Sherrin and James Gilbert." There seems to be no reason to question this.

As we have seen, Sherrin was the man who brought Frost out of the obscurity of languishing as a trainee at Rediffusion and who, on *That Was The Week*, gave him the sort of break nobody at the commercial company felt prompted to give him. To that extent he could be said to have "made" Frost.

But after *TW3* and the follow-up series *Not So Much a Programme*, television satire had, it seemed, shot its bolt. There was a further series, *B.B.C.3*. By choice, since he felt that enough was enough, Frost was not the linkman for what turned out to be an anti-climax. He could well be thankful that his name was not associated with them.

But the American philosophy of "quit while you're ahead" is all very well if you have something to go on to. Frost did not have anything specific on the books and in 1965 he went into what now on reflection can be called a lean period. In the autumn of 1965 he appeared on the Eamonn Andrews show. Viewers were interested to see him there. "Good heavens, there's David Frost!" It was one of his few appearances on T.V. in that period.

It was then that James Gilbert came back into the Frost orbit. Gilbert, one of B.B.C. television's top comedy producers, went to the Montreux Festival with Michael Bentine in 1963. As producer and star, they were there to keep their fingers crossed for the B.B.C.'s entry that year – the best of *It's a Square World*. The show did not win the top award, but it did get the Press prize. Coming back on the plane, they celebrated this consolation award with champagne. Also on the plane was Frost and, before the celebrations were over, Gilbert had suggested to him that they get together to discuss a possible new series.

It was in this chance-meeting way that the programme that was to be the highly successful *Frost Report* was born and the way the format was decided on was just as fortuitous. When Gilbert and Frost did put their heads together in 1965 to try to evolve a good idea for a series, they felt that it should include the best nightclub acts in Europe. With this as their somewhat vague blueprint they went off together on a tour of the capitals of the Continent in search of cabaret talent.

"Paris, Amsterdam, Brussels, Copenhagen . . . " Gilbert recalls. "Scurrying around to all the night spots. We were soon nightclub punch-drunk. But it was in Brussels that we got the nub of the idea. Why not take a different subject each week of the programme and do tongue-in-cheek documentaries on it? When we got back Antony Jay was commissioned to write thirteen essays on a variety of topics – the Countryside, Advertising, Holidays, the Armed Services, Education and so on. They were quite serious essays, but not without wit.

"These essays we had run off and copies given to a group of comedy writers we had picked for the show, for them to write sketches emanating from the material. Some of them didn't go for this, just tossed the essays aside without reading them. They weren't used to working that way. It *was* a different approach to comedy writing. But I thought it was a good plan. It's tough to say to a comedy writer, 'Write us something funny,' just out of the blue like that. I felt they had a starting point with each of those essays and, as it turned out, eventually they all came around to it."

Frost's spiel was prepared separately from the rest of the programme – the pieces of specially filmed material and the studio sketches into which it was interwoven. Frost would go away to write his own pieces and edit the copy produced for him by the team of writers and Gilbert would not learn what Frost was going to say on the programme until they got together in his dressing room a few hours before the live twenty-five-minute show went on the air. Gilbert purposely delayed on this. "It was so that I could bring fresh ears, as it were, to material that a lot of people had done much work on and I could regard it objectively. I would make suggestions for cuts, which were easy enough to do, because it was intentionally written too long and Frost could readily make adjustments to it. In the margin he had them all marked First Division and Second Division jokes."

Frost's sense of participation is such that, as well as being linkman, he wanted to take part in the sketches with Ronnie Barker, John Cleese, Ronnie Corbett and Sheila Steafel. Gilbert had to dissuade him from this. Gilbert feels, like others, that in the field of performing in television skits, which reaches its apogee with Peter Cook and Dudley Moore and is done superbly by Ronnie Barker and Ronnie Corbett, in that category Frost is not as talented as he is in the chair. But Gilbert had to do his dissuading obliquely, pointing out to Frost that there were some 12,000 on the agents' books fighting for the acting parts that were going, whereas there was a bare handful in the linkman field; why compete with the many when he was so successful among the few? Frost was convinced. Gilbert had probably done him a great service.

The telephone directory aspect of the credits which used to go on the roller after each *Frost Report* was the subject of many a snide comment. For example, *Private Eye*: "Janette Scott was included on the grounds that she might possibly have thought up half a joke." *Private Eye* had it only half right. Credits *were* given for a contribution of merely one joke. Jimmy Gilbert says: "Frost is a brilliant editor. He would go through scripts picking out bits here and there to get together the talk he would be doing between the sketches. Sometimes he would take one line from a whole script. The writer wouldn't care about the guinea he would get for it, but a credit as a contributor to the Frost show – that really meant something to him."

That was why the writers were unhappy when Pye Records brought out an L.P. of the *Frost Report* in February 1968 and no writers' credits whatsoever appeared either on the record label or the sleeve. "Just a mistake," says Gilbert, a mistake that was rectified when the contributors made their annoyance public. The record itself showed little sign of emulating the T.V. show's success. Listening to it, one felt that it just didn't work, not in the same way that a Shelley Berman, say, or a Bob Newhart record does. Berman and Newhart are purely verbal comics. One doesn't need to see them in action and indeed nothing is gained if one does. On the other hand, so much of the *Frost Report* was visual. In fact, after listening to the record one realised that, with only a couple of exceptions, all the best parts *were* visual. Which is the very reason why it was such good television. The karate experts . . . Big Ben striking the hour . . . sports day in the prison yard . . . these and so many other well remembered skits got their roars of laughter visually. They could not be reproduced on a record. They could only be enjoyed again by being *seen* again, which indeed they were, in a special programme of the cream of the Frost show when it was shown to British viewers at Easter in 1967 and went on to win the Golden Rose at the Montreux television festival a month later.

The idea of doing a portmanteau edition of the show and convincing the B.B.C. that it should be submitted as their entry at Montreux came to Gilbert and Frost in a pub just before closing time. "David certainly called the shot on that one," Gilbert recalls. "As soon as we had the idea he pointed to his watch and said, 'You will never forget this day, it will be imprinted on your mind, because it was today at five minutes to three that we decided to win the Montreux award for Britain'." Gilbert can't remember when it was exactly, but he still remembers the elated confidence of Frost that they would win when he did a jig outside the pub.

The gratitude Frost felt towards Jimmy Gilbert showed itself in tangible form. Shortly after the Golden Rose of Montreux was proudly put on display by the B.B.C. in the lobby of their Television Centre, Gilbert received a gift from Frost – a replica of the Golden Rose.

"The interesting thing about it," says Gilbert, "is that it is a better job than the actual award itself. The real one has a wooden base. David's replica has marble. The golden rose itself made by Asprey's, done by hand, whereas the Montreux people churn them out from a mould. The price must have been quite staggering. But that's David."

The Frost Programme, which had its first airing on 28 September 1966, was a natural development of *Not So Much a Programme*, which had had a talk-and-sketches formula. Now the sketches were out and it was primarily a talk programme, with interludes, usually musical. Frost became much more serious. He emerged in the role for which he had, knowingly or not, been grooming himself and which is undoubtedly his real metier – the television interviewer.

On ground prepared for him by such people as Ed Murrow in the States and John Freeman in England, Frost flourished to such an extent that in the field of television interviewing he has proved himself the ultimate professional. In his twenties he is sadly showing up his elders. Men such as Malcolm Muggeridge, whose concept of interviewing is a four-paragraph question calling for a one-line answer; Bernard Braden, who has about as much warmth and contact with his audience as Harold Wilson; Eamonn Andrews, who as the years roll by has shown such a resistance to learning how to interview people that it is probably true to say of him that never in the history of television has so much been paid to one man to come up with so little; Robin Day who might well learn from Frost that a very useful ingredient for an interviewer to have is humility.

The Frost interviewing technique, some of it consciously developed, most of it naturally evolved, has several other key aspects of which ambitious newcomers in this field should take careful note.

Although viewers may not be conscious of this until it is now brought to their attention, Frost differs from other interviewers in that he always goes after Number One. For instance, if it is a controversy about Defence – get the Minister of Defence. If you can't get him, don't do it. Don't settle for his deputy or other "official spokesman". And never sink to the next, worst alternative – an "expert" on the subject, who is invariably one of the over-exposed Fleet Street political writers who do the rounds of all the discussion programmes expounding their conjectural, "outside" opinions on any given topic. ("We have in the studio Perigrew Westhorn, who *tonight* is an expert on statistical anthropology.")

The illustrative story on Frost's insistence on getting Number One concerns one of his staff being despatched to Rome to line up an interview with exiled King Constantine of Greece. The staffer phoned back to say that it couldn't be done. "All right," said Frost, "we'll scrap it. But as long as you're down there, get the Pope."

Something else which helps to make Frost consistently good television is that he rarely has women as interviewees on his programme. This is borne out by observing that in the table of contents of *Playback 1*, the book of interviews of the first series of *The Frost Programme*, the forty-three interviewees consist of forty-one men and two women. Unlike others who conduct talk programmes, Frost is wary of the fact that women on such shows seem to have an inborn ability to be a cause of irritation and embarrassment to viewers. In television, except where femininity is prerequisite, the female personality does not come over well, as evidenced by the fact that women as newsreaders have been tried and abandoned, and it is just unthinkable to have a link*woman* for such programmes as *This Week* and *Panorama*. Frost put it in a nutshell when asked why he so seldom interviews women: "If they decide to be feminine they tend to sound unintelligent, and if they decide to be serious they tend to lose their femininity."

Another rule in the Frost interviewing textbook which could well be called *How to Win Viewers and Influence People* is: Never plough doggedly through a list of prepared questions. Frost has his prompt sheet on his lap during an interview but on it are "areas I feel it would be worth while exploring" rather than fixed questions. "I'm more interested in conversation than interrogation. Interviewing somebody can be so boring. I've been interviewed myself by people who have their little set of rigid questions that they are painstakingly ticking off one by one. I feel like saying, 'Oh, by the way, I've slept with the Pope's wife'. Because I'm sure they'd go right on to the next question, 'What about the adverse balance of payments?'"

A classic example of this plodding-on-to-the-next-question type of interviewing occurred on the Eamonn Andrews show when George Raft was one of the guests. Raft told Andrews that there had been a period when he was in grave financial trouble and when he mentioned this to Frank Sinatra one day, Sinatra said, "All right, George, I'll lend you a million dollars". Eamonn Andrews merely turned to Dora Bryan and said: "Have you ever had any money troubles, Dora?"

And Frost has come to learn, early, that the use of rehearsed "tough" questions, the type of aggressive interviewing indulged in by some interviewers, does not necessarily produce good television. "That sort of question," he says, "is the easiest of all to duck. If you thunder at a government leader, 'Isn't it true that your party has spent two years in self-serving policies?' then you'll get a lousy answer. But if you ask casually, 'What is the major mistake your party has made since it has been in office?' you challenge the man, and he'll respond with something interesting."

In illustration of how being aggressive is not always the best way for an interviewer to get the most out of a person, Frost likes to quote the Aesop fable about the sun and the wind having an argument about which of them could make a man take his coat off. The wind blew and blew and the man just turned his collar up tighter. Then the sun came out, all warm and soft, and

57

the man took his coat off and everyone could see what he was like.

Frost used the soft approach in his interview with George Brown – unexpectedly in the minds of many viewers, who thought he would go at him, with resultant fireworks. But afterwards Frost felt that he had got from Brown much more revealing frankness ("I don't want to be Prime Minister; I don't believe I've got what you need to be a Prime Minister") with gentle questioning, and this was borne out by what Brown remarked during the interview: "It is odd to be discussing things as frankly as this with you in front of an audience and cameras."

Frost's interview with Defence Minister Denis Healey was the direct antithesis, with both at each other's throats. Henry Fairlie has said: "Whatever else television has done, it has introduced into every home in the country the habit of listening to argument." Frost versus Healey, on the subject of Defence cuts, was the epitome of this.

Frost says now that he had not intended it to be a battle. "But Denis Healey came to the studio spoiling for a fight. He said he had had raging toothache all day. Perhaps that had something to do with it."

It is still one of his most talked-about programmes and it was one of the few occasions on which Frost seemed to be caught out of his crease. He was seen to use the audience more than once when the going became rather rough for him, using the interviewer's trick of getting a guest to repeat a statement which he knew the audience would pick up: Healey: "Harold Wilson is infinitely the best Prime Minister we could have." Frost:

"Pardon?" Healey: "He's infinitely the best Prime Minister we could have." Laughter. Voice from audience: "We must be hard up." Laughter. At the end of the programme Frost unconsciously acknowledged this help he had had from the audience when he departed from the usual order of precedence in giving his signing-off thanks: "There we must leave it. Thank you audience. Thank you, Minister. Goodnight."

Healey scored against Frost by countering Frost's use of interviewer's tricks of the trade with his own tricks learned from years of experience as a political campaigner. When confronted with several questions rolled into one he picked out the one he wanted to answer and avoided the rest. ("Could I answer your major question, which is the really important one . . .") When Frost said that "people" were saying such-and-such he demanded to know which people, putting Frost in difficulty over being specific. From time to time he sought opportunities to take command of the interview away from Frost. ("You'd better turn to another question." "No, we'll stay with this one.") With throw-away lines, he did his best to plant in viewers' minds the feeling that Frost was merely the mouthpiece of a team. (". . . Your researchers haven't reminded you of that.") And by his frequent use of "Oh, really, David," he made use of a technique described by Robin Day in his book *Television: A Personal Report*: "Skilled politicians are always careful to flatter the interviewer who asks awkward questions by a casual reference to his shrewdness and intelligence, or by being very friendly towards him. On *Panorama* one night Mr. Iain McLeod used my Christian name ('Well, of course, Robin, as you know . . .'), thus taking the sting out of a sharply critical question. The television interviewer must be on his guard against such legitimate, but undermining, tactics."

Frost's summing up of the Healey encounter: "To the extent that it was a contest, I would say that he won the first half and I won the second. But why make it a contest at all?"

The Labour Party definitely felt it was a contest, and it was a matter of such Government concern that a transcript was flown by special plane to Harold Wilson who was in the Scilly Isles at the time, for him to decide whether "anything may call for legal or other action". As it turned out, no action was taken, since the Prime Minister, along with many other viewers, had misheard Frost. He had not asked Healey to divulge Cabinet secrets. He had merely questioned him about newspaper stories to the effect that he was in favour of the sale of arms to South Africa, to find out whether the stories were true, or were just another example of Fleet Street's famous El Vino conjecture.

In an article they ran on Frost, *Life* magazine said: "If you ask one of his detractors the logical question, 'Just what does David Frost have?' the answer comes back with a snap: 'Nothing, but he does it better than anyone else.'" And Thomas Thompson, writer of the piece, went on to say: "What Frost does have is the ability to put someone at ease and just talk."

He was able to get Lord Thomson of Fleet to be revealing about how he got his peerage ("When I want something everybody knows about it; I talked to the people that mattered") and why he wanted it so much ("When I was born in Canada of very poor parents, there wasn't one chance in a thousand I would die a peer in England. And my God, I've made it! That's accomplishment, isn't it? That's why I wanted it.")

He got Hugh Cudlipp to reminisce about his early days at the *Daily Mirror* and call to mind the best head-line he ever wrote: "There was a boxer called Lee Oma, and Peter Wilson, one of our splendid sports writers, wrote a story about him. It appeared to Peter Wilson that Lee Oma, the great heavy-weight American fighter, fell down in the fight and lay on his back rather soon. So I put a headline on it in very large type which said: 'OMA COMA AROMA'."

A. J. P. Taylor expounded an interesting theory when asked by Frost whether he agreed that this was possibly the worst set of politicians we have had this century: "It would be a very bad day for us when we admired our politicians. The Germans enormously admired Hitler. And look where it got them. The Italians thought Mussolini was wonderful. The Russians thought Stalin was wonderful. The great virtue of a democracy is that it always thinks its leaders are frightful. And it's an even greater virtue of a democracy that they are always are! That is what we have democracy for. If we were really cursed with inspired, wonderful leaders, think where they would get us."

Frost got Colonel Mike Hoare, leader of mercenaries in the Congo to confess: "My officers came to me and asked me to try a man for murdering a Congolese girl ... We decided we would pass sentence on him, although we weren't a properly constituted court ... We had discovered that this fellow was a professional footballer. So I decided the best thing to do was to pass sentence that his big toes were to be blown off. So we took him down, and he was screaming and yelling, and we did it. I took out my Colt revolver and shot his big toe off each foot."

He got Mick Jagger, pop-grouper and convicted drug-possessor, to admit to also being a hero-worshipper. "You're a lot of people's hero, Mick. Do you have a hero of your own? Someone you look up to?" "Eamonn Andrews."

Frost's interview with Ian Smith was a prime example of what has been described as "the new telediplomacy". It was a coup of the type pioneered by Robin Day ten years previously. In 1957, Day's interview with President Nasser six months after the Suez crisis was referred to as "nation speaking to nation in a new way". James Cameron wrote in the *News Chronicle*:

Sitting in the garden of his Cairo home, President Nasser leaned forward last night into British television screens.

And he asked that we reunite in friendly relations.

He thus did something that had never been done before in the history of international diplomacy.

For the first time on record a national leader submitting a major point of national policy, by-passed all protocol and sent his message into the homes of another state – *at a time when the two were not in diplomatic relations.*

Frost was likewise able to convince the leader of a country with which Britain had broken off diplomatic relations that he should state his case direct to the people of Britain by television, by-passing the Prime Minister and other diplomatists who were without question very attentive viewers of *The Frost Programme* that night. Frost had got the interview with Ian Smith very simply. He had merely phoned Smith, to find him receptive to the idea. After the programme Frost gave a press conference for diplomatic correspondents eager to develop the story, since Frost had momentarily moved from communicator to participator in events. It is a heady situation when a reporter finds himself the central figure in a matter of such great concern to the public. He is in the position, even fleetingly, of knowing more about what's going on than those directly concerned. Frost, as with others to whom this has happened, relished it. But at the press conference Norman Hoskins, Press Officer of Rediffusion, soon had to step in and cry, "No more! No more!" The publicity for Rediffusion was great. But telediplomacy was showing every sign of getting out of hand.

Frost has had on his programme what *Life* called "an extraordinary roster of big names", but there was one programme of unnamed guests which made absolutely compulsive viewing for the simple reason that it abounded what is known in the trade as "viewer identification". We were all once children and a high percentage of us now have them, so when he assembled an audience consisting entirely of children he was half way there before the show even started. His premise: "During this series there have been many occasions when adults told us what they think children think. But they don't really know. It's always the adults talking about children. But tonight we thought the children should

63

talk about the adults, or anything else they wanted to talk about."

They talked, eagerly, about various well-known adults. Harold Wilson, for instance. "He keeps on spending our money on things which should be going to other things. Like this submarine, this atomic submarine. He took all our money for it. It cost thousands to make, and then when they put it in the water it just leaked." Sir Francis Chichester. "He sails in sailing boats on rather dangerous trips, and I think he's going to kill himself." Quentin Hogg. "My opinion is he is too old to work."

And they talked about God and the power of prayer. "I think you should be allowed to say what you want really in prayers and not just a silly poem that you don't know what it means. You should be able to talk to him as a person." "I don't think prayer works at all, otherwise those children in the Congo wouldn't starve." "Teachers are always telling you that God thinks of all people as equal, whatever colour their skins. But he seems to help the wealthiest business tycoon in England or America; in one night they pray in their minds that their business deal will go through the next day, and the next day it will. It may be just a coincidence, but God doesn't seem to be helping the children in the Congo." "Those children are born who have done nothing at all, and then well, the death rate in the Congo used to be one child every three minutes, which is an awful rate for them to just sort of pop off. Born into the world and immediately just disintegrate! I personally think that that means there is no God. Otherwise they wouldn't be starving. There would be plenty of rice, plenty of food,

64

Arriving at a charity performance with Jenny Logan

Frost at a recording session with fellow *TW3* star,
Lance Percival.

plenty of clothes. No drought or locusts or anything."
"I don't think you pray for 'Stop this, stop that'. I think
you pray to God to forgive you for doing things you
shouldn't have done."

The freshly scrubbed youngsters in their best suits and
dresses, bright-eyed and alert, came through as wonder-
fully unaffected television performers, thanks to the
ability of Frost to handle children, showing genuine
interest in them and never talking down to them.

He loves children, even if through his repeated assertion that he is not going to marry until he is in his thirties
he has no inclination to make an early start on having
some of his own. Betty Munro, child psychiatrist, has
said: "He may be less good with children on television
when he does have his own. At the moment all his love
of children is poured into children in general. When he
has his own children he will become comparative. 'This
youngster's very bright. Same age as my Richard. Is he
brighter than Richard . . . ?' "

Chapter 5

Strictly Personal

David Frost runs one car, a metallic bronze Mercedes which cost him £4,500. He drives it himself, fast. Peter Cook has been heard to say: "Have you ever driven with David in his Mercedes? Hair raising!" George Brightwell has reached the stage where often as not he will say to Frost: "You go on ahead, David. I'll follow in a taxi." Frost enjoys driving alone, since it gives him a chance to get away and think. He especially likes driving after a programme. It helps him to get his mind clear, where he thinks things went wrong, where he'll get it better next time. But he doesn't drive on any trip that will take more than an hour. He feels that beyond an hour it is no longer relaxation and he prefers to go by train or plane and get some work done *en route*, as on the two and a half hour train journey from London to Beccles, Suffolk, to visit his mother. He is one of the select four hundred people in Britain who have a phone in their car and it is probably his favourite toy. An expensive toy. It costs £200 to have one installed and whereas ordinary subscribers pay 2d for a six-minute local call, Frost's calls from the Mercedes cost 1s 3d for three minutes. Incoming calls are drawn to his attention by what the Post Office calls "a discreet buzzing" and the flashing of a light on the dashboard. It is a radio phone and the handset looks like the mike of a tape recorder. Frost's is pale blue with a red knob at the top to manipulate for the over-to-you-Roger-and-out routine. His secretary, Joan Pugh, finds it a mixed blessing. "I just can't get the hang of the over-to-you business." His agent, Diana Crawfurd, also finds it frustrating. "It's no good for a woman," she will tell you with a smile. "You can't interrupt. David controls the conversation with that little button on the thing. But I will say that when he makes a joke he does say, 'Over to you for laughter'." The phone is restricted to use within Britain, and Frost would be happier with his toy if he could make trans-Atlantic calls. Talking to New York while speeding up the M1 would be to him, one feels, living to the full.

He lives in one of a terrace of Regency houses in Egerton Crescent, along the road from Harrods. Although the South Kensington tube station is just a couple of streets away, the district is known as Knightsbridge. This is the idea of the estate agents, to up-tone the address to keep it in line with the prices they charge for leases – from £15,000 to £25,000 according to the condition of the house. Frost's is in very good condition.

Of the narrow, vertical type in vogue when it was built more than one hundred years ago, it has a basement and three floors. The front door is a beautiful thing of teak, the sort of door that could cost £100. It sets the pace for what is to be found within.

On the ground floor is the dining room and a kitchen which appears to have every type of gadget known to kitchen science. The dining room table is an oval expanse of marble of such size that it has to be placed diagonally for the room to accommodate it, and then only just. There are numerous paintings, dominated by a big canvas which explores a subject dwelt on by an earlier artist – sun-flowers. But one knows this is very modern because "John Bratby 1967" is writ large in one corner. A similar painting by the same artist has been on display at the Marlborough New London Gallery, priced £400.

In the basement there is a Scalectrix racing car layout which any boy might feel that, not in his wildest dreams, could anyone actually own. It is like one of those really grand ones set up for demonstration in a toy department. With extras. If your business with Frost is not too pressing, you are likely to wind up down there in the basement, which is often one of the focal points of parties in the Frost home.

As you soft-foot it up the lush plush red carpeting of the staircase you are flanked by William Morris wallpaper hung with abstract art by a modern whom anybody will excuse you for never having heard of – Peter Sedgley. And you find the first floor almost entirely devoted to one big combination drawing room-study-office.

In contrast to all the technicolour downstairs the mood here is predominantly black-and-white. White ankle-deep Indian carpet to the walls and black leather couch and armchairs. There is an indoor version, in chrome with black upholstery, of the type of elongated reclining chair seen in the best appointed gardens. On the walls are blow-ups of monochrome photographs; one, big enough to be a mural, is an aerial shot of downtown New York by night. There are standard lamps in profusion, the main eye-catcher being a hooded light on the end of a parabolic arm which can be swung around to any position in the centre of the room. Frost will tell you that he chose everything in the house himself. "I don't believe in interior decorators," he says.

As striking relief to the black-and-white theme is the Orange Bomb, a chair of the type one sits inside rather than on. Frost was among the first in London to have one and he imported this one from Denmark. Encased in this womb-like ball, glistening orange in colour, you can swing around to view all points of the room. It needs oiling.

On the mantelpiece above the fireplace is a strange admixture of cups and other awards, soccer vying for attention with television. The soccer trophies include several connected with the Showbiz XI, for whom Frost was a regular star until his expanding activities cut down his appearances for them. The television awards represent the highest one can go as far as accolades are concerned – Television Personality of the Year through to Show Business Personality of the Year, the Richard Dimbleby Award and, in pride of place, a replica of the Golden Rose awarded at the Montreux Television Festival.

One should not feel that an insight into character can be gained by a study of the books on the shelf on one side of the mantelpiece, where an Agatha Christie stands beside *The Religions of Mankind* in a display of reading matter that ranges from Steinbeck to Brian Inglis on *Private Conscience and Public Morality*. Frost has little spare time for reading books. Many of his friends and

69

others send him ones they have written in hopes of publicity.

The shelf on the other side of the mantelpiece is an array of bottles of every conceivable type of hard liquor. But one should not draw false conclusions – Frost doesn't drink.

There is hi-fi equipment which is a magnet to any guest interested in that type of thing and the records include, unexpectedly, "Selections from *Carousel*" and others of that ilk.

At the end of the big room that looks out to the patch of garden is Frost's desk, which is so vast that it has a west wing. On the wall beside it there is a Geochron, the sort of timepiece which no member of the Jet Set should be without. It is an American geographical chronometer ("Geo-chron – get it?" as Frost would say in the forward-leaning, semi-sinister form of delivery that he has made his very own television trade mark). It consists of a map of the world, with a back-lighted portion that moves across the face of the earth as time goes by, enabling you to see where the sun is shining and know what time it is at any given spot on the globe. It is an extremely useful gadget to have on hand when phoning through to San Francisco or Rhodesia to arrange a hook-up for his programme, although Frost's secretary says she has yet to see him consult it.

In Frost's home one cannot readily detect a television set, since it does not occupy the key position for T.V. addicts in the corner of the living room. Frost is not an adherent of the Noel Coward maxim: "Television is for appearing on, not for watching." He enjoys viewing but does not get a great deal of time for it.

One feels that Frost's Spanish housekeeper, Luisa, is type cast. Short, full-bosomed and volatile, one would swear she has been playing Spanish housekeepers in films for years. Frost says of her: "She would be great to have around, even without the hundred and one things she does. She makes me roar with laughter." She is from Madrid but has lived so long in England that she now talks of how "we" have to put up with "our" weather. She never ceases to marvel at the fact that Frost never loses his temper. In domestic crises, such as her forgetting to send to the cleaners a suit he wants to wear, she will be prepared to let loose her Latin temperament in an altercation, but it never comes. "Control, control," she says shaking her head as someone of a race to whom it is quite foreign. "He is always under control."

Her thrifty background is at odds with Frost's habit of turning on lights. "As soon as he comes into the house he will turn on every light," she says, "even if it's still daylight outside." She mentioned this once to a guest who dabbles in psychiatry and his explanation was that Frost, brought up in the household of a Methodist minister where pennies had to be watched, had probably been told constantly to turn off lights and now, making so much money that he could be termed rich, he turned them on all over the place to compensate for the strictures of his youth. "That may be so," said Luisa, "but when he's gone to bed I still have to make a tour of the house in the middle of the night turning out all the lights."

John Wells said of this: "It's not just a matter of his now being able to thumb his nose at the electricity bill.

Insecurity, that is the thing. There must be loads of light. One cannot face the dark."

Peter Cook: "My wife and I have been at his home, lights blazing, when it gets to be three o'clock in the morning, four o'clock and still he is reluctant for us to go. He just doesn't want to be left alone."

Frost's personal secretary, Joan Pugh, is an attractive, well-groomed young woman, married and with children in boarding school; she has the enviable knack of being able to remain unruffled in the wide-ranging turmoil of Frost in action at all hours of the day and night. Not the least of her headaches is coping with more than 1,000 fan letters he receives each week. He likes to deal with these personally and never delegates the signing of replies. "People seem to regard David as a sort of one man citizens' advice bureau," she says. Letters can range from "How can I get my son out of the army?" to "When I became pregnant I bought a pram. I have now had twins. The shop will not take back the pram in part payment for a twins' pram. It is not really adequate for twins. What can I do?"

Frost did not in this case send the poor woman a double-size pram, although it is the sort of thing he is likely to do. He is generous, which is not necessarily the case with all who come to be well off through their own hard efforts. One of England's best known self-made tycoons, for example, thinks nothing of returning home from a trip to Europe with a half-pound carton of delicious Belgian chocolates for a close friend. Frost frequently makes thoughtful, by no means inexpensive, gifts to people he does not know well but to whom he feels for some reason he would like to make a gesture.

Whenever he visits his mother in Suffolk he is always laden with gifts; a new car for Christmas was not an out of the way present for him to make her. He never arrives as the guest in someone's home without bringing something, especially things which will please the children of the household. On the Christmas before he went off to America to promote his new book he gave a party in his home for the people connected with his programme. With friends, plus gate-crashers, it amounted to some 150 people. Everyone, including unexpected arrivals, received a gift. From Aspreys.

His generosity extends to spectacular parties thrown at the end of a series. When the first *Frost Report* series drew to a close in June 1966, Frost hired Battersea Fun Fair for an all night party for four hundred people. Items such as overtime pay for staff who had to be kept on after the Fun Fair had closed to the public helped to boost Frost's bill for a night of fun and games in and around the round-abouts to £2,000. His party after the *Frost Report*'s 1967 series was on an even larger scale and earned for him the nickname of "The 20th Century Nero". He rented the White City Stadium for the evening, its 35,000 seating capacity making every allowance for gate-crashers, as one wit who received an invitation remarked. The guests were regaled with a lavish dinner, followed by egg-and-spoon and three-legged races and other of the non-Olympic branches of athletics and culminating in a soccer match in which their host participated.

Frost stands 5 ft. $11\frac{1}{2}$ inches tall and when he broke into T.V.'s big time he weighed 12 st. 7 lbs. His weight has since gone up or perhaps one should say forward. Without drinking beer he has achieved the sort of waistline increase usually associated with the ardent beer drinker. Those who like to make snide remarks about him say that he has moved into goal for the Showbiz soccer XI because he is too fat to flourish in the forward line as he used to. In point of fact his move to goalkeeper was as far back as Cambridge, when he didn't have enough time to train.

He has an indoor complexion. John Wells has said of him that "he is one of the few people I know who can go off on holiday – and come back looking worse than when he left".

He has a deep sense of loyalty and this extends to his clothes. Secretary Joan Pugh says he will wear a suit until it drops off him. His suits are off the peg and conservative, blue is the popular colour, worn with brown suede shoes. He was mystified when he was named fourth Best Dressed Man in an *Evening Standard* poll – ahead of Cary Grant and Lord Snowdon. He is not a sharp dresser, nor is he trendy, except to the extent of his being one of the first in London to embrace to the full the polo neck vogue and in New York was sufficiently ahead of his time to be refused admission, with Lord Snowdon, to a fashionable restaurant for being tieless.

But he went for polo necks because they are practical in a busy world, rather than to be a pace-setter. He has no real interest in clothes, in the same way that he makes no great fuss about food. If you ask his housekeeper what his favourite dish is she will say: "Chocolate biscuits." She despairs about the fact that he eats them to keep himself going when she is only too willing to prepare full meals for him at any time. He does not like highly seasoned food, which rather puts a damper on her spicy Spanish ideas. "He is a country boy and likes simple food," she says. Guests at his house invariably have to ask for mustard, since he prefers not to have it around. This dates right back to a bitter memory of one day in Kempston, Bedfordshire, when his mother left him in his pram outside Brinklows and he delved into a whole tin of Colman's. In a restaurant he is likely to be less interested in the food than the people who are there. He is one of London's leading table-hoppers. He has no favourite restaurant where celebrity hunters can rely on seeing him. When dining a girl he often uses Parkes, in Beauchamp Place, where food comes adorned in flowers and one way and another it is big romantic stuff. He frequently takes business associates to lunch at the Ritz on a Saturday because things are so quiet there on Saturdays that one can talk in unjostled comfort.

He likes to breakfast out, invariably at one or other of London's better hotels. Ever conscious of his figure, he says his regular breakfast is melon and two boiled eggs. "But occasionally," he says, "I slip in a sly mushroom and bacon." He is a great adherent of the working breakfast and much of his business is transacted over the breakfast table. Fitting in breakfast appointments with people who want to see him about some deal he occasionally finds that his early morning guests can have conflicting interests and this means that he has to have two breakfasts at different hotels. "When that happens,"

75

Frost says; "I have the melon at one hotel and the eggs at the other."

Besides doubling up on his breakfasts (he has been known to have three working breakfasts in one morning when the pressure is on), he also doubles up on business meetings. On one occasion in his house he had two meetings going on at once in different rooms. They were quite unrelated, one being about an American T.V. show he was preparing and the other about a charity appeal. Like a chess master tackling two boards, he alternated between the two.

Once, he was able to get the Prime Minister to have breakfast with him. Slightly more lavish than melon and eggs, the menu featured grapefruit, bacon and eggs, sausages, kidneys, tomatoes and mushrooms, toast, pots of coffee – and champagne. It was in the Carlos Room at the Connaught Hotel in Mayfair and besides Mr. Wilson there was a guest list of notables that included Lord Soper, the Methodist leader, and the Bishop of Woolwich, Lord Longford, then Colonial Secretary, David Astor, editor of the *Observer*, Cecil King, Kenneth Adam, Director of B.B.C. television, Len Deighton, Patrick Campbell and Robert Maxwell. At a cost of £150, Frost was said to be reviving a breakfast fashion of Victorian times, when in the 1880s it was a regular occurrence for such gatherings to be held around the morning meal prior to getting down to the work for the day. Guests at Frost's breakfast, which was from nine-thirty to eleven o'clock, were reluctant afterwards to discuss what went on, since it was a private affair attended by the Prime Minister, but one did reflect the

76

wide-ranging aspect of the guest list by commenting that it was "a curious affair".

When, a few weeks later, Frost held a similar gathering for Mr. George Brown, the Deputy Leader's co-guests included his wife Sophie, Lord Devlin, Leslie Caron, Robin Douglas-Home, Bryan Forbes, Clive Irving and Robert Maxwell. Although he had intended to make it another breakfast on the lines of the gracious living of Victorian times it was eventually changed to a dinner party.

The letters Frost writes, apart from those to the Archbishop of Canterbury, say, or the Prime Minister, when one has to watch it a bit, are always very informal. They are likely to end with "Greetings!" or "God be in your feet". His secretaries have learned to be alert to the fact that he will call for dictation at any time or place – at breakfast, after a late-night T.V. show, in his Mercedes doing 100 up the M1. His flights to New York being so frequent (Freddie Ross: "Flying to the States, to David, is the day trip to Southend."), he uses the time for clearing his ever accumulating correspondence. Joan Grimwade, who was his personal secretary before switching to David Paradine Productions, has been on several of his "dictation flights". On these trips he is what she terms "a non-stop dynamo of work". What happens is that she is booked on the flight with him and takes along an empty suitcase. Among his luggage is a suitcase full of letters, scripts, business reports and other paperalia. One by one, as she burns up the shorthand notebooks, these items are transferred from his suitcase to hers. On arrival in New York he goes off about his business and she catches the next plane back to London, with the suitcase. At £296 18s. for her return fare, it is a fairly costly way of doing the equivalent of an eight-hour day of dictation.

But of course, much of his paper-work is taken off his hands by his agent. Frost is fortunate in having Diana Crawfurd as his agent. She is a good-looking young woman, smartly turned out. But when the contract discussion is at its height she is tough. Although it was not said of her but of somebody else, she is "the steel marshmallow".

She has the intense loyalty to Frost that all ten-per-centers have to those of their clients who are the jam on their bread and butter, for Frost at the moment is their big money-spinner. But by the same token Frost is loyal to Diana and her associates in the well-appointed rabbit warren that is Noel Gay Artists Ltd.. He has never had any other agent. He is lastingly grateful to them for the fact that when he was a little known writer first arrived in London they pushed his writings around to all the papers and worked at making sales for him, unlike other agents who can have a tendency to take only a token interest in the striving authors on their list and devote the bulk of their time and thought to their established writers, dead and alive.

Diana thinks back to the old days and remembers how excited Frost was when she was able to present him with his first fat cheque. He left the office and hailed a taxi to take him to be measured for a new suit . . . and kept the taxi waiting outside with the meter running. For Frost it was like the comment of the negro grave-digger who saw an eccentric millionaire being lowered into his grave at the wheel of his Cadillac with a 12-inch cigar in his mouth: "Man, that's living!"

Now, of course, he can afford to keep taxis waiting not only on special occasions but whenever he feels like it. The Frost lateness is well known. For him, twenty minutes late is good. An hour late is not exceptional. Anne de Vigier, the part-Swiss actress who had her first just-friends picture with Frost in the papers in October 1967, says of his lateness: "I always take a book along when I'm going to meet David. I know I'll have time to get through a couple of chapters before he arrives." But his is not the annoying type of lateness when one knows that the person concerned has nothing else to do but be on time. Frost running late throughout the day is akin to a dentist, who starts with the best will in the world not to keep his patients waiting but delay on one appointment spills over into the next and the cumulative effect is a crowded waiting room. Few people show annoyance at Frost's lateness because invariably they are there to get something out of him.

His girl friends don't mind waiting for him. Frost's name has been romantically linked with certain women with whom he has been seen in public. These include Jenny Logan, Janette Scott, Charlotte Rampling, Julie Felix, Carol Lynley, Anne de Vigier, and Rita Faria. All, save Beauty Queen Faria, are in the entertainment world. And all have been told that he does not intend to marry until he is thirty, or thirty-five, depending on when they came in.

When Janette Scott flew to New York while he was working there, newspapermen smelt romance in the air and she revealed a nice sense of humour when she told them that the purpose of her visit was "to buy a refill for my mother's pen, a ballpoint from Tiffany's." Harried by English pressmen on her return, she was asked about time spent with Frost, "Are you going to marry him?" "Why should you suppose that?" she replied. "I saw the Beatles when I was over there too, but I'm not marrying them."

Pictures of Janette Scott in the nude appeared in *Town* magazine and the Charles Greville column of the *Daily Mail* felt convinced that the Earl Wallerman whose credit line appeared with the pictures was a *nom de photographie* of David Frost. When confronted with this, Frost said: "It's a mystery to me." Quite understandably, since he had never been known to have any interest in photography and his association with Clive Labovitch, the then editor and joint-publisher of *Town*, is merely a business one concerned with the broader aspects of magazine publishing.

Frost's mother and father were very taken with Janette Scott when he took her up to see them at Beccles. And when, after two years of saying "We are just friends", she did marry, but not David, Mrs. Frost was sorry to learn the news. "We hoped he would marry Jan," she said in a rare interview. Friends felt he was visibly cut up about it, the first real indication of a weakening in his non-marriage plans. But Frost says the break-up was mutual.

Private Eye carry on a running feud with Frost, but they will hasten to tell you at the magazine that although

With producer James Gilbert, showing the Golden
Rose of Montreux awarded for the 1967 programme,
Frost over England.

How an idea is born.

Frost, then editor of the magazine *Granta* and in his last year at Cambridge, leads a debate as guest speaker in the Cambridge Union.

they are feuding with him, he is not feuding with them. They call him Gypsy Dave, for no special reason, and as one of their favourite targets they seldom let many issues go by without at least one jibe at him. He achieved some sort of record when he received ten separate mentions in their first issue of 1968. But it was in their issue of 29 May 1964, that they had fired their biggest single barrage at him. It was a full-page profile headed "The Bubonic Plagiarist, or There's Methodism in His Badness". After describing one of his programmes, the piece went on to say:

"A few knowledgeable eyes began to flutter when the credits came up at the end.

"For the eyes, beneath astonished fluttering eyebrows, saw in large letters the message: 'Script by David Frost.' They blinked and looked again. The obliging technicians kept the words on the screen. Yes, it really did say that. Then came the qualification – 'with special material by', followed by a list as long as your arm. This was quickly removed. (After all, names like Muir and Norden are too well known to need additional plugging.)"

Analysing the sketches in the show, *Private Eye* came to the conclusion that a take-off on *Sportsview* "was obviously the only sketch bad enough to be written by Frost." And they continued: "But surely it had said, and, come to that, didn't it say in the *Radio Times*, 'Script by David Frost', and assuming the analysis to be correct didn't this constitute what could be described as a BLOODY GREAT LIE?

"Indeed someone wittily remarked that after the show four hundred people phoned the B.B.C. – three in favour, four against and three hundred and ninety-three to say that they wrote the script."

The profile then went on to give alleged examples of Frost using material in his cabaret act and elsewhere without giving credit to the originators, and concluded with the comment that he should be content merely to be "a good compère and take his place between Peter Haigh and Macdonald Hobley."

Private Eye have good reason to say that they are carrying on a one-sided feud with Frost. Shortly after this broadside they were sued for libel over another matter and numerous well-known personalities in the entertainment world got together to put on a show to raise money for them to fight the action. Frost was only too glad to contribute his services.

Numerous *Private Eye* writers who over a period of years have, anonymously, attacked Frost have been hired by him to write for and perform on his shows. This faculty he has for turning the other cheek has merely elicited from *Private Eye* the unrepentant comment: "Jesus Christ was the David Frost of his time."

Frost shields his mother from the limelight. He has a deep affection for her. He does not want her to be pestered by reporters and magazine writers. ("Mrs. Frost? This is *Woman's World* calling. Were David's first words 'Goo goo' or did he say something brighter?") She has granted only one newspaper interview, which was sprung on her rather than granted. In 1966 a reporter and photographer arrived from London, unannounced, on the doorstep of her Beccles bungalow and she was gracious enough to let them in. It has not been allowed to happen again. A feature writer who suggests to Frost that he talk to Mrs. Frost to round his article out will receive a charming smile and "Let's leave Mother out of this, shall we?"

When one does meet Mrs. Mona Frost one finds her a warm-hearted, jolly person, grey-haired, wearing glasses. She was born in the village of Darsham in Suffolk, no great distance from where she now lives in Beccles, in the bungalow her son bought for her. It has under-floor heating and big picture windows which look out across the flat fields that surround the somewhat bleak town. Beccles is no great centre of industry but it does have two printing works. Not long ago an employee of one of them, William Clowes and Sons Ltd, met Mrs. Frost in the main street and said: "Do you know what book we're printing now?" "No," said Mrs. Frost. "Your son's book – *That Was The Week That Was.*" Which is the pleasant sort of coincidence that pleases parents, especially when page proofs are smuggled out for an advance peek at the book.

Beccles is in the Anglia T.V. area, which was rather frustrating for Mrs. Frost. When *The Frost Programme* was launched in London, Anglia T.V. was not among those of the provincial outlets which networked it. So she was in the unhappy situation of having her son making headlines with his programme while she herself couldn't see it, except at such times as she visited a Frost-conscious television area. She wrote to Anglia T.V. and they were very nice about it. They put Frost on for her. But not the full programme each week – only those of his broadcasts that didn't clash with wrestling.

83

Frost visits his mother every week when in England, phones her each week if abroad. Unless he has a Saturday broadcast he makes the 109-mile trip to Beccles and if he takes one of his "young ladies", as Mrs. Frost calls them, the three of them watch television on the Saturday evening and go to church in the morning. There is nothing much else to do in Beccles.

As soon as Frost arrives in the bungalow he says to his mother: "I've got to make a phone call." The phone call invariably develops into a batch, many of them to America. At first Mrs. Frost, accustomed to a life of watching pennies, got the horrors at the thought of her phone bill, interspersed with such items as half-hour chats with New York. But now Frost pays it for her. His personal phone bill is never below £1,000 a year.

She has never kept a scrapbook of her son's doings (his is a vast, several volumed affair, kept up to date by secretary Joan Pugh) but she had a fair collection of photographs. One of them she prizes very much is of David with Princess Margaret and her family in the garden of their home. The picture carries a comment from Princess Margaret to Frost: "You seem to have an effect on my son because he looks so serious."

Mrs. Frost was terribly pleased when her son made *Who's Who*, in the 1967 edition. Not the first television personality to do so, since Gilbert Harding, Richard Dimbleby and Cliff Michelmore had preceded him, but certainly the youngest. And she was thrilled to hear a couple of months later that in that other field of recognition of the famous, Tussaud's, they were seeking permission to put the callipers on David for a figure to take its place beside the only two T.V. men currently on view

84

at their exhibition, Cliff Michelmore and Eamonn Andrews.

Mrs. Frost worries about her son's health. "You're overdoing it. Five hours sleep is not enough." She tries to get him to have a session in a health farm. She feels he doesn't get nearly enough exercise. She tried to get him to go for walks but gave up when he said: "Me strolling around London? People would wonder what had got into me."

She keeps up steady pressure on him to take a holiday. He has taken only two holidays since getting into the big time – one to Majorca and the other to Crete. In the bar of the Pension Santa Margarita in Paguera, Majorca, there is a notice: "David Frost Stayed Here." Gwen Kelliher, English owner of the *pension*, says that visitors want to be shown the room he slept in and sit on the same stool where he drank. "It's quite uncanny," she says. However, the hotel in Crete where Frost stayed has not similarly been made a shrine. The owner, being Greek and not *au fait* with British T.V. stars, didn't know when he was on to a good thing.

Frost has never owned a dog and his disinterest in dogs stems from the fact that his mother would never have one in the house. "They make a mess." But Frost has on occasion found himself involved with female dog owners. "It is a bit awkward for him," says Mrs. Frost, "not being used to them around the place and then one of his young ladies has one. I remember him bringing a girl up to Beccles for the weekend and phoning me ahead of time to say, 'There's a poodle on the way.' It was thoughtful of him to warn me." Some of his friends feel that it is unusual for him not to have grown up as a boy with a dog or even wanted one. Richard Ingrams once remarked: "You can't take a car for a walk – but David tries."

Mrs. Frost is still active in the Church. She is Vice-President of the Methodist Women's Fellowship, she trains the ladies' choir, and also she does a great deal of sick visiting. All of this helps to keep her busy, which is a good thing, because her son worries about her now that the Rev. Frost is no longer there. The frequent phone calls she gets from London invariably end: "You *will* tell me if you're lonely, won't you."

Frost's father died at 9.15 a.m. in Beccles. Frost had an important luncheon engagement in London that day. He kept it. It might have seemed callous to dash off and leave his mother up there at a time like that. But both his sisters were in Beccles and his mother and he decided that he must go. The lunch, which consisted in its entirety of warm wheat grain and milk with fish protein biscuits, was the typical meal of starving millions in India and Frost was there to launch the Oxfam Christmas Appeal. The exhorting speech, press interviews, posing for pictures and all the other hoopla of a charity luncheon . . . "I don't know how I got through it," he said afterwards.

For Oxfam he flew out to India at his own expense on a fund raising trip. His detractors hasten to point out that while there he had another talk to John Freeman about joining London Weekend T.V., but the interesting thing is that the detractors have not themselves flown to India for Oxfam nor been in the position to enlist Freeman. One of his knockers once said of him that "he has a convenient social conscience." But few people know of the time and money he devotes to the after care of prisoners; he has visited Parkhurst and Broadmoor to talk to the inmates. Nobody until now has read about the fact that he supports a family whose father was tragically killed. There are other examples of furtive generosity.

His father's funeral was on a Thursday and when Frost returned to London to do his evening's broadcast his colleagues on the programme were surprised at his reply when they asked him about the funeral. "We had a wonderful time," Frost said.

"They just didn't understand," says Mrs. Frost. "His father had a lingering death. An active man who lived life to the full, whom David was so close to, it was so sad to see him like that towards the end. We could only feel thankful when he was taken. At the funeral David said: 'Father is at rest now. Let's make it a happy funeral, for his sake.' And it was a beautiful funeral. The singing afterwards and everything. It was such a wonderful atmosphere."

One is likely to see parked outside Mrs. Frost's bungalow an Austin 1100, de luxe model, with radio, heater and all other trimmings – a surprise Christmas present from her son. "He had given me the most wonderful presents that Christmas," Mrs. Frost recalls. "All sorts of lovely things, a beautiful outfit, a Methodist hymn book, the very latest with a zip fastener. And when he said he had another present for me. 'It's next door,' he said. And as we went around he stopped at a car outside the house next door. He had had it driven up from London. 'Jump in, Mother,' he said. 'It's yours.'"

He paid the £60 for her driving lessons, which she

took at the age of sixty-three. He wanted her to be able to drive so that she could take her husband out for rides in his declining years. Oddly, Frost didn't get his own driving licence until he was twenty-six, after several brushes with traffic police which included being in court for driving without L plates. "My fans stole them," he explained. The magistrate was understanding. Mrs. Frost, urged on by her son, passed her test at the second try, which was not bad going for a woman in her sixties. She has set some sort of fashion in the area for older women to take up driving, under the tutelage of a very good instructor in Beccles. A woman of seventy-one recently got through her test, which is the present record for East Anglia.

The Christmas gift of the car was followed a couple of weeks later – Mrs. Frost's birthday is in January – by a present of a splendid electric lawn-mower which keeps the lawn behind the bungalow immaculate. Bringing up David and his two sisters on her husband's stipend, which was less than what a London bus conductor earns, was, she admits, "a strain". How many women having, willingly, done all that for their children are fortunate enough eventually to be showered with good things and be asked, "Is there anything else you want, Mother?"

On one of his many trips to New York, Frost was interviewed by a reporter with regard to Britain's dire financial situation. "Is it possible now," he asked, "for a person starting off from scratch to make a million dollars?" Head down, pencil poised over his notebook, the reporter became conscious that the answer was rather long in coming. He looked up to see Frost smiling. "Ah!" said the reporter. "I get you!"

Whether in fact he has earned the £418,421 11s. 3d. required to qualify as a dollar millionaire is a secret between Frost, his accountant and the tax inspector. But he has certainly come a long way up the financial ladder since starting from scratch as a television learner in 1961.

His £20 a week with Rediffusion at the outset got a quick lift to £135 a week when he was taken on by the B.B.C. to do *That Was The Week* in 1962. When he did *Not So Much A Programme* he was upped to £600 a week – three shows each week at £200 each. Interwoven with these were his appearances in the American version, for which he received $850 for one programme per week, a figure which was trebled when he did his second series in the States. This rising tendency continued through *The Frost Report* which followed and by the summer of 1967 his rates of pay were increasing so rapidly that it became a subject of national concern. With a Freeze on, a question was asked in the House as to whether the fact that I.T.V. had announced they were going to pay him £20,000 for three months of *The Frost Programme* was a matter for the Prices and Income Board. Apparently it wasn't, and Frost's pleasant financial spiral continued when 1968 opened for him with the American network, the Westinghouse Broadcasting Corporation, assigning $300,000 for him to do the first series of four one-hour television shows for them, his take from the package deal being undisclosed.

All that, of course, was merely the money he was making from television series. Constantly it is augmented handsomely by his fees for one-shot appearances, his book royalties and earnings from other writing, cabaret appearances, directors' fees, investment income and all the other addenda which come with hitting the jackpot in the entertainment world.

However, one lucrative source of revenue he has turned his back on. Although others in his sphere of television have done T.V. commercials – Peter Cook (beer) and Bernard Braden (soup) – he has never done any. When *That Was The Week* was at the height of its popularity and "You're doing a grand job" was the catch-phrase of the moment, someone in an advertising agency got a brilliant idea for plugging a medicine that was one of their accounts. Frost would hold up the product and say to it: "You're doing a gland job." The agency was quite hurt when Frost turned down this proposition. But even though at that time he could have used some of the generous fees advertisers pay his attitude then, as now, was: "The reason I won't do commercials is that I would never say anything I don't believe in."

One can only guess at what all his varied efforts bring in for him in terms of financial reward. A friend has said he now earns £60,000 a year. It could well be that he earns considerably more. He certainly doesn't earn less.

The bonanza has enabled him to live in style in his town house, even if some of his friends are rather blunt in their views on it. "Completely lacking in taste." "Ghastly." "I'm convinced that's not where he lives at all. He must have a pad somewhere." As yet he hasn't a country place to go with his town house. He has done nothing as yet about a private yacht. But, as someone remarked, there is time enough for all that.

When the Frost yacht does ride gracefully at its moorings in the Mediterranean it is almost certain that it will be called *Mona II*.

Chapter 6

Frost in Action

The Frost show all starts, of course, in the conference room. The conferences early in the week are devoted to broad planning – what's in the news, who'd be good to have on this week? Conferences held on programme days are concerned specifically with each of the chosen guests, exploring their background, lining up what they will do or be asked about.

Frost's team usually consists of twelve advisers, editors, and researchers. They have been alluded to as "the witty parasites" and "the scintillating sycophants". They were called "ex-Fleet Street, ex-wonder boys" by Hunter Davies, the new Fleet Street wonder boy. But this is not fully accurate because some of them are Oxbridge products, such as Neil Mellersh who, like Frost, came straight into T.V. from university; Antony Jay, who gets considerably more yardage later in this book; Ian Davidson, who came to Frost through revue and B.B.C. satire writing; and John Penycate, bright young researcher.

Fleet Streeters who have been prominent in the Frost team are Clive Irving, whom everybody in the magazine world knows or knows about; Peter Baker, former Deputy Editor of the *Daily Express*; Neil Shand, erstwhile *Daily Sketch* gossip columnist and now earning a closed-circuit reputation in the T.V. trade as provider

92

of laugh material; and Peter Noble, who hovers between Fleet Street and Wardour Street, darling.

By virtue of the fact that it entails mainly sitting around trying to be bright it is an odd, new sort of way to earn one's living, the type of job that is not yet sufficiently crystallised for a school leaver to say to his careers master: "What I want to do is to be trained for a T.V. personality." An observer might feel sorry for them, sitting there trying to be creative on somebody else's behalf and wishing to hell that they were earning recognition in their own right. But at £30 to £100 per week, according to stature, one needn't feel sorry for them, especially as they all have other irons in the fire and are occupied in this way only when their employer has a series on the air or is in gestation.

Frost's detractors are fond of saying that he is merely a front man for a team. But so are Managing Directors, Cabinet Ministers, and others when they give a performance which involves making a speech with facts and figures prepared for them by their staff and like as not polished up and with nice little humorous touches added by one of their P.R. men.

Bennett Cerf tells the story of a dignitary who didn't even bother to read the speech prepared for him before going on to the platform. He came to a passage which started, "Which reminds me of one of my favourite stories . . . " He had not heard the joke before and laughed so much at it that he broke his glasses and somebody else had to read the rest of his speech for him.

But there *is* a difference between Frost, along with other team-fronters in television, and the man in business or government who gets the backroom boys to provide the material to make him sound good. In the latter case, the "team" of department heads and other staff who assemble the ammunition for the boss do it merely as an adjunct to their main work in the organisation. Frost's team is brought together and paid exclusively to supply his needs. While at work on his shows it is a full-time job for them.

There is an interesting comparison to be drawn here between television stars such as Frost and similar performers in print – the newspaper columnists. Frost has a huge advantage over, say, Bernard Levin in his capacity as columnist for the *Daily Mail*. Levin has all the facilities of the *Daily Mail* at his disposal – the reference and cuttings library, the newsroom and wire room, and other sources of material. But these are merely shared facilities. He does not have a team of twelve who meet each day to do nothing but think up and develop ideas for him. The newspaper columnist does the bulk of his work by the sweat of his own brow. In contrast the "T.V. journalist", which is what some people call Frost, has it laid on a platter for him.

In those terms it would be correct to say that Frost is derivative and synthetic. But those who say "Who couldn't look good with all those people behind you providing you with stuff?" overlook the fact that it does not follow that a front man for a team is automatically good. The failure to shine or the outright failure of numerous television people with teams behind them just as energetic as Frost's is evidence enough of this. Delivery, personality, ability to ad lib – these and other attributes of the front man make the difference between whether all the preparation is put to good or bad use.

94

The crack about Frost that "he does nothing but does it better than anyone else" is glib, but it has the nub of truth.

If you are invited to join one of the 10.30 a.m. conferences for the Frost show and arrive on the dot of 10.30 you won't find much action. You can have breakfast, though. It is laid out on a table in the corner – rashers of bacon, buttered toast, rolls, ham, marmalade, jugs of coffee, and milk on a hot-plate.

The huge conference table, a twenty-seater, is strewn with that traditional source of ideas for others besides television men – newspapers. The eight conferees who have already arrived sit around the table making themselves bacon sandwiches, sipping coffee, and scanning the papers. Conversation is desultory. After half an hour the complement is brought up to fifteen; as well as Frost's ideas men, also on hand are the show's producer, director and the studio floor manager, plus three secretaries. Frost has not yet shown up.

When he does breeze in, he apologises, "I was accommodating a *Sunday Times* photographer," and opens up his briefcase at the head of the table.

The conference comes alive.

Conferences, in any field of endeavour, can be of two basic types. On the one hand the boss is completely dominant and those along the table each side of him are merely yes-men, aiming to please him, hoping to impress him. And at the other extreme, the brains are really with the key men along the table and the boss, spongelike, just sucks up their ideas and is thankful that they

95

are going to make him appear very capable. A Frost conference is mid-way between these two.

Those who would like to think that Frost is just a brain-picker with little to contribute himself would be disappointed to observe that it isn't so. But by the same token he is not so strong on ideas that the members of his team are merely tributaries to his main stream. He is more the catalyst in a free-for-all throwing around of ideas.

Except when the subject necessarily calls for some serious pondering, he keeps everything light-hearted. He feels that conferences should be fun and enjoyable. Some might get the impression that a Frost conference can become frivolous. But it is a planned policy of kicking subjects around, saying anything that comes to mind, even if corny. Out of many a facetious crack has come the nub of a good workable idea. Some conferences elsewhere take themselves so seriously that their lack of sparkle is reflected in the end product. A Braden conference is conducted much more efficiently. Bernard Braden is incisive. He knows what he wants and is quick to channel ideas along the lines he feels they should go. His show is no longer on the air.

As well as the inter-passing of ideas at a Frost conference there is discussion of the mechanics of putting the programme out, how many minutes each guest will have, the running order, and other technicalities.

The director announces: "Gracie Fields wants an hour in make-up."

Frost: "I must read some biographies of Gracie Fields. I'm just a young lad. Thoughts on Gracie, please."

The Frost Programme on the air.

With George Brown, then Foreign Secretary.

At a Foyles literary luncheon in December 1967, with co-author Antony Jay and Scottish Nationalist M.P., Mrs Winifred Ewing, to mark the publication of the book *To England With Love*.

In the dressing room after a charity soccer match.

In his own drawing room.

"She's lived so long in Italy now that she toks like theez."

"I Took My Mandolin to a Party."

"Gracie Nostra."

There is much use of "area", the new word that has taken over from "level", as in "What area should we get Dick Gregory on to?" Frost shows his fondness for "at this moment in time", which is American for "now".

Somebody offers him a cigarette and he takes it mechanically. A light is proffered for him, since he carries neither cigarettes nor matches. Later he is seen to be smoking the cigarette held between his teeth, sure sign of someone who is not really interested in smoking.

Frost: "What are Bob Newhart's causes? Has he got any causes?"

"I haven't heard of him having any."

"I don't know that he's any good at talk."

Frost: "He's going to feel rather hurt if we just get him to do his submarine bit and then not get him to talk. Someone find out what he can talk about."

There are two phones by the wall near the secretaries. They ring frequently and from time to time Frost is called over. Leaning against the wall, he talks quietly on the phone while the conferees continue to confer, like a tribe without its leader. Frost gets some of the calls transferred to the phone out in the lobby of the conference room; some business matter which people on the programme needn't necessarily know about or a girl friend; nobody can eavesdrop, anyway.

Back at the conference . . .

Frost: "What poetry will we get Betjeman to read?"

"How about him reading some lyrics as poetry? I've heard him do it and it works."

"Are there any Gracie Fields numbers that can be read as poetry? Then we could kill two birds."

Frost: "Do you think we've been a bit soft lately. Should we get Dick Gregory to be serious?"

One of the studio staff who is present expounds an idea at some length. He is listened to with interest. His voice betrays that he didn't go to public school.

The conferees make intermittent visits to the buffet as breakfast becomes morning coffee and waitresses come in with replenishments.

Frost: "Thoughts on how we can use the audience tonight."

"I've got a wonderful idea for getting us off the air. Tied in with Backing Britain. Gracie singing *Land of Hope and Glory* backed by the band of the Grenadier Guards and the audience all waving Union Jacks."

"I think flags of convenience would be better."

"Excuse me, where's the flag of convenience?"

Around one o'clock inspiration is beginning to peter out, dead horses are starting to be flogged, so Frost winds things up with a run-through of who has to do what to get the programme thoroughly organised, and then suggests that they all meet again at five o'clock.

The editors go off, each to prepare his list of questions to the guests from which Frost will add to his own and make his final selection. The researchers go off to delve into the books and the cuttings and to do phone-arounds. And the advisers go off to think up some more advice.

They all report back at 5 p.m. for the final conference

before the night's programme. All the loose ends are tied up and then it's over to you, David, and out.

Frost usually arrives at the studio at nine forty-five for the programme going on the air at ten thirty. But he is just as likely to arrive as late as ten past ten, by which time the director and others concerned with the transmission are starting to show signs of anxiety. But when Frost, still in his topcoat, strolls in he is quite un-ruffled – "the complete T.V. pro", as they say of him. He talks with the technicians about the mechanics of that particular show, which of the numerous chairs he'll do each interview from, where the various props will be placed. There is no run-through, no rehearsal. There is a pile of scripts on a chair. If you are naïve enough to pick one up you will see that the first page of the half dozen sheets of yellow foolscap bears the mimeographed names of the producer, director etcetera, date, and time of transmission. The remaining pages are blank.

Having satisfied himself that everything in the studio is under control Frost goes off to talk to that evening's guests, who are standing by in the hospitality room. The studio audience is already assembled, except for vacant seats marked RESERVED in the two front rows. These are now occupied by friends of Frost and others con-nected with the programme, and by people invited to be in the audience because of their specialised know-ledge or interest in the subjects Frost will be discussing with his interviewees. Some can be seen to be consulting their notes to make sure that if singled out by Frost for some audience participation they will get their off-the-cuff comments straight.

The audience having now been brought up to its full complement of two hundred and twenty, the warm-up man comes on to get them in the mood. This he does by telling jokes, all of them near-the-knuckle, most of them old. They are always the same jokes, numbered 1 to 10. The audience chooses them by calling out numbers. Number 3 concerns Robin Hood and his Merrie Men about to hold up a coach. Robin Hood says: "I want you to rob the women and make love to the men." One of his band says, "Surely you have that around the wrong way." Comes the high-pitched voice of another of the Merrie Men: "He's our leader. We'll do as he says." After nine more in similar vein the audience is ready, eager, for some worthwhile entertainment.

Meanwhile, in the hospitality room . . .

This is a hard place to find and perhaps intended to be so. Many a would-be free loader presumably gets lost in the numerous corridors trying to find the tiny staircase that leads up to it. The large room has at one end a huge "directors' special" T.V. set – a two-screen panel with elaborate controls. Beside it is a bar, with white-jacketed barman. There are some easy chairs. Little else. Except people. It is always jam-packed because, as far as drinks are concerned, the price is right, as the saying goes.

Frost, who has an office just along the hall, pays only a brief visit to the hospitality room before the show. He has nothing to drink, smokes only if someone happens to offer him a cigarette.

He has a short chat with each of the programme's

guests. To Gracie Fields: "Shall we talk about Rochdale . . . ?" To Peter Ustinov: "That bit of yours about the difference between an American, a Russian and an Englishman standing on a street-corner . . . " It does not seem to be a very thorough preparation for the show, but it is not really as casual as it appears. Frost and his team have been in touch with each guest beforehand, working out topics. Nevertheless no rigid line of questioning, no fixed form or shape is laid down before going on the air. The only thing that is planned is that each interview will appear unplanned.

A make-up girl comes in to check the guests. "What about your make-up, Mr. Ustinov?" Peter Ustinov runs his hands over his cheeks. "I put it on this morning as usual, isn't it all right?" People in earshot laugh. Except the make-up girl. She looks as though she has heard the joke before. Often.

A reporter or feature writer is probably somewhere in the mêlée, there to get some sort of story from Frost. He is very good copy, the most consistently newsworthy of all the T.V. performers. A couple of photographers are likely to be clicking away, getting candid shots of Frost and the people he is talking to, while mini-skirted girl friends of lower-rung executives of the programme jostle to be glimpsed in the background of the pictures.

A cluster of salesmen congregate around Frost, eager to sell him some ideas or themselves. "See you after the show," he says, hurrying off to his office for a last minute chat with his producer.

He emerges with the interviewer's crutch, his prompt sheet of questions and lines of discussion, and enters the studio to a round of applause which he acknowledges with a wave and a smile as he goes to his chair or, if there is time, with a short speech to the audience: "Thank you for your support. I shall always wear it."

He shows no nerves whatsoever, which is not necessarily the case with all compères and interviewers. Eamonn Andrews, for example, though not nervous within himself, is ever fearful that someone is going to drop a brick and his studio presence puts one in mind of the George Jean Nathan comment that a certain actor "played the King as though he were in constant fear of someone playing the ace". The suave Bamber Gascoigne delayed the start of one recorded edition of *University Challenge* when he dropped all his questions and had to re-assemble them in the correct order. Gilbert Harding used to be so nervous that he exuded brandy flavoured perspiration.

Producer James Gilbert, who has been dealing with stars of theatre and television all his working life, says that they all show nerves one way or another – but not Frost. "He is a unique animal," he says. "When things go wrong he never goes into a flap. He seems actually to welcome it. He enjoys the challenge of getting things out of the mess."

There is the now well-known example of the mynah bird that was one of the world's great talkers – until brought on to Frost's show to prove it. Not a peep. No matter how hard Frost and the bird's owner tried, not a word would it utter. Frost didn't get flustered. He launched into an ad lib routine and finally with a laugh he shrugged his shoulders to the audience. And then turned to the bird. "Can you come back next week?"

An interesting contrast is how Simon Dee handled,

or rather, mishandled the same situation. A talking budgerigar on Dee's programme likewise refused to co-operate. Dee got rattled. He shook the bird's cage, exhorting it to talk. A thing he should never have done. Quite rightly he brought down upon himself a deluge of letters from lovers of our feathered friends.

Watching Frost from the studio audience one realises just how polished his delivery is, especially when it comes to laugh lines. Thomas Thompson, feature writer for *Life*, says that "most of Frost's jokes are so old that it is a toss-up which of them was the one Queen Victoria was not amused at". But they get over. When Walter Winchell was asked why he rattled off his newscasts so quickly he said: "So many of the items are stale that if I deliver them at high speed nobody has time to notice they're old news." Although with Frost it is not a case of high speed delivery, he has, nevertheless, evolved his own technique for putting across a high percentage of jokes which have been around a fair while. James Gilbert says: "His timing is immaculate. He sends demand notes out to the audience for laughs."

Elkan Allan has said of Frost: "He is the greatest T.V. pro. He was born in a television studio."

He is in his element getting his teeth into a serious interview or more lightheartedly moving around the studio – "That lady there, in the blue dress . . ." He does not affect the blasé sophistication of the compère who would impress you with his importance; Frost has the exuberance of a kid at his first pantomime.

And when he says, "Good heavens, time is up already, I didn't realise – talking to you has been so enjoyable," it is not a signing-off gimmick. He means it.

103

In the hospitality room afterwards the drinking pace quickens now that the pressure is off for those who had the transmission of the programme on their mind. Frost comes in and sets about seeing the people whom before the show he promised he would see. Orange drink in hand, he goes from one to the other in turn. He listens attentively, head down, taking in every word. Each one he talks to obviously has the satisfying feeling that Frost is interested in what he is saying. In this respect Frost differs from many people, successful in the entertainment world, who have the disconcerting habit of looking not at but past you, with the look in their eyes that says, "Don't change the subject, you were saying goodbye." People coming away from meeting Frost for the first time have a tendency to say, "What a nice person he is."

Associates of Frost who are not necessarily among his well-wishers will tell you, "Oh, that's just part of projecting the Frost image." But this does not take into account the fact that more than a few performers known for being likeable on stage, T.V. or radio don't bother to let the image spill over into their private life.

Wilfred Pickles does not number many old age pensioners among his friends when not on radio. Bernie Braden surprised a friend he was lunching with when a young Canadian introduced himself to Braden and said he had just come over to try his luck in television here – and Braden gave him the freeze, with the explanation, "Why should I help him? He could take work away from me." Danny Kaye in person has been known to disappoint admirers of his screen image.

The faculty Frost has of being genuinely interested

in people pays dividends on his programme. Because of it, he gets more out of his guests than the run-of-the-mill interviewer does. The edition of his programme that was devoted to children was a good example. He was able to make them talk, fascinatingly, because they felt that he was interested in what they had to say. They were so caught up in his interest that they lost their self-consciousness and eagerly came back at him with questions, such as, "Why do you bite your nails while the commercials are on?", a question which took Frost unawares. (He has since let his fingernails grow.) With adults Frost's natural inclination to be interested in the other person has resulted in this situation: politicians, and others who consent to be on his programme, confident that they can deal with anything this whipper-snapper is likely to throw at them, find that he becomes so engrossed in what they are saying that they become interested in his interest in them and they say far more than they ever intended to when they accepted his invitation to appear.

Meanwhile, back in the hospitality room . . .

The lushes have achieved that pleasant free-liquor glow, the young executives have, they hope, got their dollies into a receptive mood, the secretaries on late-night duty are yearning to get home and their shoes off, salesmen who have been trying to sell Frost on something are saying to themselves, "Let's have lunch some time and discuss it," is not nearly as good as, "Let's have lunch on Tuesday, 12.45, at the Ritz." . . . There is a nod to the barman. The shutters are down. Frost, around whom it all revolves, has decided to go.

When he leaves the studios Frost gets into his Mer-

105

cedes and drives to the West London Air Terminal in the Cromwell Road, just a few streets away from where he lives. His call there on his way home is to see the man who has a newspaper stand in the arrival hall and from whom you can buy tomorrow's papers ahead of time. He always has a set of the national dailies for Frost, who pays him a retainer for the service. In this way Frost is able to start at once on getting ahead with his next show without having to wait until the papers are delivered in the morning. Actors in West End plays, and others interested in finding out as soon as possible what the papers have to say about them, do this more laboriously by going to Fleet Street and doing the rounds of each newspaper office to get advance copies. Frost gets his papers in one fell swoop. "Trust David to have that organised," a friend once remarked.

Chapter 7

Trial by T.V.

When the *Sunday Mirror* exposed insurance tycoon Emil Savundra and the *Daily Mail* exposed Dr. John Petro, no police action was taken.

But after David Frost interviewed Emil Savundra on his television programme, Savundra was arrested, tried for fraud and sent to prison for eight years. And when Frost interviewed Dr. Petro he was arrested while leaving the television studio, tried for drug offences and fined £1,700.

On the face of it, one could assume that television interviewer David Frost has more power and influence than the Press. After these two now famous "trials by T.V." many viewers did indeed come to the conclusion that Frost had got action where big newspapers had failed. But it was not as simple as that. It did not take into account the fact that when the alleged wrong-doing of an individual is exposed the police are not necessarily in a position to go straight out and arrest him. Considerable investigation and preparation of the case against him must be undertaken before they can proceed.

Police preparations in secret for the arrest of Dr. Savundra and of Dr. Petro were well advanced when Frost interviewed them. It was merely that the timing of the interviews made it appear that Frost had galvanised the police into action.

Whether or not television, in the form of Frost, had more influence than the Press, it was clearly shown to have more impact. When the *Sunday Mirror* and the *Daily Mail* published their exposures of Savundra and Petro there had been no public outcry about "trial by Press". The reason for this is that when stories of that nature are carried by a newspaper they are edited and re-edited, gone over with a fine toothcomb by the newspaper's legal department, even vetted by the subject if he makes it a condition of his giving an interview that he checks the quotes attributed to him. There are dozens of safeguards against libel and contempt of court.

But Frost is live television. The man concerned is there in the studio in person, now. The interview is as unscripted and un-edited as the proceedings in a criminal court. It has all the appearance of a trial – and breaks practically every rule laid down in the tenets of British justice. The interviewer is at once judge, prosecutor and jury. He does not follow the rules of evidence, asks leading questions, puts words into the "defendant's" mouth. The man "on trial" has no legal representative to tell him what he should and should not say. He can call no witnesses in his defence, though the interviewer calls witnesses for the prosecution, in the shape of people planted in the studio audience.

The interviewer would appear in all ways to be "usurping the functions of the judiciary".

Newspapers were quick to point out that if they did the same sort of thing they would be charged with contempt of court and they asked: "Is there one law for T.V. and another for the Press?" But more than one paper came out in support of Frost.

Under the headline, "Don't Stop the T.V. Trials!" in the *Daily Mail* Peter Black, best T.V. critic in the business, wrote: "The fact is that a broadcasting organisation must accept that some T.V. ought to be live. Having done so, it must accept that such T.V. is uncontrollable. The B.B.C. principle is to train producers to take decisions for themselves and when in doubt ask the next man up. This is the healthiest way to run a T.V. service. Even if Lord Hill wanted to control it all (and there's no sign that he does) there is no team of lawyers in the land that could draft instructions for producers that wouldn't bring programmes to a halt. The only waterproof instruction would have to be: Don't do anything."

Philip Purser wrote in the *Sunday Telegraph*: "I would not mind if angry viewers besieged Frost's studio, or if everyone left in England refused to go on the show, or if someone punched him on the nose on the air. I would be incensed if officialdom tried to prevent him from running such risks. The fact remains that the crusading (or, if you must, muck-raking) tradition is an ancient one in journalism. If you inhibit it at the seedy end, how can you be sure it will survive at the level where it convicts the Messinas, exposes E.T.U. ballot-rigging or forces the Crichel Down enquiry?"

That, however, is merely comment. What of the three authorities to whom the public could look to take any necessary actions against "trial by television" – the government, the law and I.T.A. (controlling body of the channel which broadcast the Frost programmes)?

On 27 February 1968, the whole question of trial by T.V. was debated in the House of Commons. The report in *The Times* next morning was typical and the headline as misleading as those carried by most of the other papers:

"TRIALS BY T.V." TO BE BANNED

Both the B.B.C. and I.T.A. have given assurances to Mr. Short, Postmaster-General, that they will prevent "trials by television". Mr. Short told the Commons last night that he did not believe statutory safeguards against such programmes were necessary or desirable.

"I know that some sort of voluntary code of conduct will emerge from the discussions I have had with them."

During an adjournment debate reference was made to the Savundra and Petro cases.

"Both Lord Hill (of the B.B.C.) and Lord Aylestone (of the I.T.A.) have themselves told me that they were acutely concerned that programmes of this kind might become a form of trial," Mr. Short said, "and that justice might suffer. I know that they are determined to see that this is not allowed to happen. The best safeguard is the assurance I have obtained from them that they will see to it that it does not happen again."

Mr. Alexander Lyon, Labour M.P. for York, who initiated the debate, said he had no desire to criticise Mr. David Frost, who had contributed much to the development of television in his own way. But, Mr. Lyon said, he should not entertain by conducting a trial.

Our Broadcasting Correspondent writes: Mr. Short's announcement took executives in the I.T.A.

and the B.B.C. by surprise. The I.T.A. board have already discussed *The Frost Programme* and are to discuss it again, probably this week. As a result of this meeting, informal guidance will be given to the programme companies.

The Times Broadcasting Correspondent was indeed right in saying that I.T.A. and B.B.C. executives were surprised to learn that their organisations had assured the Government that trial by T.V. would not happen again, since, for some time afterwards, there was still no official statement from either source that definite steps had been taken to put an end to that type of interview. Enquiries revealed that such a statement was not contemplated. "Trials By T.V. To Be Banned" could hardly be regarded as an accurate piece of headline writing, even if it did assuage those up in arms about the matter, as was obviously the intent of the Postmaster-General.

When Joe Weltman of I.T.A. was asked for this book what specific steps, if any, had been taken to stop the type of interview which could be regarded as trial by television he said they had not made a commitment "to see to it that it does not happen again".

"You do not solve the problem of a hot potato by cutting potatoes out of your diet," he went on. "Television is a vigorous youngster flexing its limbs. And like any vigorous youngster you must see to it that it doesn't wreck the furniture. But by the same token you mustn't stunt its growth.

"There must be live television, otherwise you are just bringing into the home canned moving pictures on

111

things past, with no feeling of immediacy or actuality. And there must be spontaneous programmes. If the Frost programme were scripted, that is, if Frost had prepared questions to which the guest provided prepared answers, why put the programme on at all, why not just have a reader saying: 'Here are the questions Frost asked and the answers he received . . .' So, given the fact that it is a free-wheeling exchange between interviewer and guests, how are you going to lay down precise instructions as to which directions the questions and answers will take?

"We have discussed this matter and it will come under discussion again at the regular meetings we hold with representatives from each of the independent television companies. That is the way we do it. We do not send out directives to producers, do this, don't do that. From these meetings we evolve the sort of guidance producers should have in the preparation of their programmes."

The feeling in legal circles is that trials by television are a dangerous development which is to be regretted, since there must be strong resistance against anything which tends towards the situation in America, where newspapers, T.V. and radio do not hesitate to do such things as referring to a man sought for questioning in a murder case as "the killer".

However, when Seton Pollock, of the Litigation Department of the Law Society, was asked, for this book, how the Law Society looked upon it, he said: "It is a tangled subject. If you impose too many safeguards you could wind up muzzling the Press and T.V., which would be a bad thing, going right against one of our

112

basic freedoms. Also it must be remembered that newspapers and television do much good work in the public interest, bringing to light many cases which call for official action and unearthing facts which are of great use to the police. However, if they overstep their role of watchdog of the public interest and become self-appointed prosecutors, they are readily brought to heel. There have been numerous examples of this. Nevertheless, it would be wrong so to hedge the Press and T.V. in with legal restrictions that they could do virtually nothing in this field.

"The concept of the Press Council is a good one. If it is felt that a newspaper has offended, each complaint is treated on its own merits. That is the common law method. From specific examples, over a long period, general principles can be evolved and a code can be formed. But it should not be allowed to harden off too quickly. It is an expensive and lengthy procedure to get things reversed and not many people are prepared to devote their time and money to clarifying the law for other people.

"The Law Society has not been asked to step in with regard to these so-called trials by T.V.. Television itself will evolve its own convention for handling such matters."

An important point about people finding themselves involved in a "television trial" is that they don't *have* to appear. In this respect it is quite the opposite of a real trial. They are free to refuse the invitation. They are not enticed on to the programme by special payment.

Savundra and Petro received merely the regular fee paid to Frost guests.

Why then, one frequently asks oneself, do individuals who know they are in for a grilling from an interviewer consent to appear on his programme – not only people likely to find themselves before the courts but politicians and others who knowingly lay themselves open to a rough passage.

The short answer to this is human vanity. There are few who can resist the temptation to appear on the box. Even if their better judgment tells them that they may come off badly, they just cannot deny themselves the pleasure of, "Saw you on telly last night", and obediently they make their way to the studio, like lemmings to the sea.

But some are not motivated by vanity. A person may feel so determined to state his case, defend his actions before the largest of all audiences, that it does not matter what rough handling lies in store for him, he's going to get his side of the picture across and justify himself.

And in the case of politicians, George Ffitch has said: "Politicians appear on television for one reason only: they think it will do them good." It should be remembered that one of the tricks of the trade for publicity-seeking politicians is this: if you give an interview to one paper the other papers won't touch it, but if you say your piece on television all the papers will pick it up.

When politicians go "on trial" in a T.V. interview, to justify their actions or attitude on an issue of the day, they are, of course, firm in the belief that they can handle any interviewer. After all, they've been through the rough and tumble of question time in the House; on the hustings they have coped with the most persistent of hecklers; at party conferences they have humbled questioners out to embarrass or denigrate them. They have had a long training at this sort of thing and it is no trouble at all to get the better of some fellow behind a microphone.

In their book *To England With Love*, Frost and Tony Jay have enumerated the ways a politician or anyone else skilled at the art of verbal shadow boxing can counter the troublesome questions of an interviewer:

"The first is the proper response to a very, very sharp question that really pierces to the heart of things. He must be able to *destroy the question* – 'That question is based on a confusion of thought. Really, there are two distinct and separate matters here. The first one is . . .' He then picks a question he would like to answer. Or he may do it more indirectly. 'That is a very good question and I would like to thank you for asking it. Let me answer it by asking you one . . .'

"He must be able to *destroy the questioner*. 'Just tell me, young man, have you ever had to negotiate on behalf of two million people? You haven't. Well, let me tell you . . .'

"He must be able to *unload the question*. If it contains any assertion or assumption, does he realise that he is supposed to forget the question and query the assumption? If the taunter says: 'A lot of people have suggested you made a mistake in . . .' the correct response is: 'Who has suggested this? Who are these

115

people? Name me twelve of them.' The taunter will then pass on to something else.

"He must be able to *make it all appear an act*. 'You know, I've come to the conclusion that I don't agree with what you suggested I should answer to that question when we were talking about this earlier. The *real* answer is . . .'

"He must be able to *use the time factor*. He must say: 'That is a very interesting question and there are nine points I would like to make in answer to this.' There is never time for nine points. So the taunter will have to say: 'Perhaps you can make the three most important ones?' and the way is then open to say with the utmost solemnity, 'No, it's far too important to answer superficially. If I can't answer it fully, I'd rather not answer it at all.'

"He must be able to *invoke the plea of secrecy*. 'There's a very good and full answer to that question, but it is involved with some things that are being confidentially discussed at this very moment. I'm afraid that's something I really *can't* talk about for another week or two.'

"And the last of the seven stock invocations: he must be able to *seek refuge in long pointless narrative*. 'Well, when I first entered public life, a good many years ago, more years, in fact, than I like to remember, my wife said to me, well she wasn't my wife then as a matter of fact. My word, no. It was a long time ago. We had both just been elected to the Worplesden Urban District Council. Well, oddly enough, the same sort of thing that you are asking about arose then. In a minor way, of course. But the principle was the same. Principles always are, you know, and I'm glad to say I haven't changed mine. Nor has my wife. At all events . . .' This secondary use of the time factor will enable him to connect the end of his rambling story in some way with the question."

The time factor is one of the interviewee's most valuable allies and anyone watching the experienced campaigner cannot help but observe how towards the end of the programme he has the clock very much in mind. When there is just a short period left before the programme must go off the air he sees to it that he is talking, and keeps on talking despite the efforts of the interviewer to stop him. "We really must settle this point before we finish . . ." He then leaves the interviewer with a scant few seconds to get the programme off the air as the credits begin to roll, and the viewer is left with the impression of him being the dominant one while the interviewer is reduced to the role of somebody involved in the trivial mechanics of hastily getting a show off the air on time.

An old hand in the field of verbal battle knows such tricks (Harold Wilson is an expert at the "clocking out" technique) and can cope with even the most aggressive interviewer. Wilson actually likes to have three people lined up against him – another little trick, in that the audience cannot help but feel sorry, even for a person whose public image is unlikeable, when three people are going at him and it just doesn't seem fair.

But, for the inexperienced guest in a T.V. encounter, everything is stacked in favour of the interviewer. In the first place, he is playing at home. He is in his own familiar surroundings. He is at his ease from the start. He has the psychological advantage that the interviewee would have if the thing were reversed and the interviewee were in his own office with his staff around him and the interviewer had to come and do his questioning there.

Secondly, the interviewer has his prepared questions, painstakingly concocted by the team for whom he is front man. The interviewee has not been shown the questions in advance, has no chance to prepare his answers and must respond off the cuff on anything that might come out of the blue.

Thirdly, the interviewer has control of the proceedings. It is he who decides which directions the discussion will take and he can channel the questions into areas most likely to be unfavourable to the interviewee. An interviewee can try to force the talk on to lines where he will show up better but he cannot get very far with this. He will find he is alienating the audience, at home and in the studio. It is the interviewer's programme. Viewers look with disfavour on anyone who comes on and tries to run the show.

Furthermore, the interviewer has the studio production team on his side, naturally. If an interviewer should fumble, be caught off guard, no producer worth his salt is going to leave the camera on him. It's switched at once to the interviewee or audience shots. And, on the other side of the coin, the guest who is flummoxed can expect the camera to linger on him. A good point made by the interviewer will be milked to the full: gleeful audience reaction shots, up sound on clapping – the sort of service the interviewee cannot hope for from a production staff whose job it is to do the best for their man.

And the interviewer, of course, has the studio audience on his side. They would not be there, were they not fans of his programme. Their mass reactions of appreciative laughter, derision and applause can be relied upon to be pro-interviewer and anti-guest. "That lady there, in the blue dress," when singled out, can be relied upon to support the interviewer and ask questions likely to show the guest in a bad light. If the interviewer is caught off guard and finds himself getting the worst of things, he can always use the audience to help him out of his plight: "Joe Blow, here, says such-and-such. Now *really*, members of the studio audience, what do you think of that!" The co-operation of the audience on these programmes can be strengthened by specially inviting a little batch of people who are knowledgeable and are known adversaries of the guest on the topics to be discussed.

The television authorities are not happy about too much use being made of these advantages the interviewer has. The using of the studio audience, for instance.

Frost, in an interview in the *Sunday Times* was quoted as saying: "George Wigg came out with that old thing about £800 million deficit being the result of thirteen years of Tory mis-rule. The minute he said it, the audience *groaned*. It was so revealing. It showed that a studio audience is valuable. In *The Week at West-minster*, which has no audience, that would have gone unnoticed, but George Wigg let himself in for it."

Being disconcerted by the studio audience was a con-

119

tributing factor to George Wigg complaining to the I.T.A. afterwards, and receiving from Rediffusion and the I.T.A. an official apology over the "shortcomings" involved in his appearance on the programme.

Another interviewer's trick which the television authorities would prefer not to be used but which is still very much in use is the Silence Technique. This is a matter of an interviewer turning to advantage the sort of discomfort all of us have felt when, as hosts at a party, conversation collapses and one pitches in with something, *anything* one can think of to say, and hears one's own voice prattling inanities. When an interviewee makes a statement the interviewer can, if he wishes to disconcert him, greet the statement with stony silence. The silence continues. The guest knows that the camera is on him, and probably even catches a glimpse of himself being inarticulate on one of the monitors. Even seconds of dead air in a studio can seem an eternity. He starts to feel foolish because he senses he is looking foolish on the screens in several million homes. So – he jumps in to fill the gap with anything he can think of and it is a certainty that what he says is going to sound as foolish as he feels.

Certain techniques which can be used by an interviewer are regarded by the television authorities as completely unfair and they have put a stop to them. One such is "the vacant chair approach". This sort of thing: "We asked So-and-So to appear on this programme but he could not see his way clear to do so." An I.T.A. executive has said: "This condemning of a person in his absence by implication is just not fair dealing and all producers know now that it will not be countenanced."

120

But perhaps it is not so much that interviewers have been stopped from doing this. It would seem that nowadays everyone is willing to appear – even if his chair becomes a pillory.

For his part, Frost says of accusations of unfair tactics: "Of course unfair television is wrong but most of the alleged practices never happen, anyway. Dr. Savundra and Dr. Petro were only two programmes out of a hundred and four, in any case. I don't think either was unfair. And remember, the audience's sympathies will always go to the underdog. So if you are going to be interviewed on television and can find someone who will guarantee to be unfair to you – accept at once. That way lies certain glory!"

Chapter 8

David Frost: Author

In November, 1967, Frost brought out a book called *To England With Love*, with Antony Jay billed as joint author. In two months the book had gone into its second edition. In the third month the publishers had to reprint again. With the gratifying disappearance of 20,000 copies from the bookshops, the publishers had yet again to get on the phone to the printers. In February, 1968, *To England With Love* was published in America as *The English*, with an initial print order of 75,000 and embraced not merely by one but by two book clubs.

Overnight, as they like to say in the publishing world, Frost had added "best selling author" to his list of credits.

On the jacket of *To England With Love* there are in all four photographs of Frost, two on the front and two on the back. There is no picture of co-author Jay. This is a fair enough balance as regards promotion of the book, since it has been the Frost image which has caused it to go so quickly from the booksellers' shelves.

Someone has said: "Tony Jay is Frost's private part." This observation, which could have been better put, brings into focus the relationship between the two men. Jay, a St. Paul's Scholar, Magdalene College, Cambridge (First Class Honours), is Frost's senior by almost a decade. His achievements have been of the behind-the-

122

scenes type – editor of television's *Tonight*, Head of Talks Features for B.B.C. television. He is extremely bright, as one is immediately aware if present at a Frost programme conference. The other members of the team treat him with deference, look to him for the penetrating comment, the apt witticism. One gets the impression that he is the Brain of those around the conference table. But he is as yet not well known to the public. His book *Management and Machiavelli* came out two months before *To England With Love* without making any great impression on the popular mind. It is a serio-comic examination of the machinations of Big Business in the light of the Machiavellianism of the 16th century, which is a bit specialised for the general reader. He is likely to become more widely known to the public through association with Frost.

Frost leans heavily on the talent of Jay. Frost needs him. But it is just as correct to say that Jay needs Frost. Frost is essentially a "public" person, not only in respect of being a performer but also in the whole syndrome of being out and about at influential parties, talked-about clubs, important receptions, well publicised first nights and all such places where "everybody" is. Jay is a more retiring type, more interested in the producing of material than in merchandising it. Frost can shop-window Jay's ideas for him.

There are some good things in the book. The section on the spending of public money, for instance, and the part dealing with education are incisive, sound comment. Also there are numerous neatly turned quips, such as the advertising man so brimming with self-confidence that "he will light a match before bumming

123

a cigarette", the assessment of English cooking ("France had Escoffier, England had King Alfred") and the penetrating observation that "the English have no unit of erotic currency of lower denomination than the full clinch".

But for those who were regular viewers of *The Frost Report* there is much in the book that is familiar. "That rich man in Chelsea who is so snobbish that he will not even drive in the same car as his chauffeur." . . . "The strange theory that you might forge a name on a cheque but never an address; that you might sign 'The Duke of Norfolk' on the front but you would always put '3, Railway Cuttings' on the back." . . . "England is proud of its export record. We probably export more scientists and doctors than any other country in the world." These and a host of other laugh-lines from the T.V. show pepper the pages of *To England With Love*.

And for regular readers of "This England" department in the *New Statesman* the book also contains much that is familiar. Katharine Whitehorn being unhappy that "a moussaka I ate in Bolton was made with potatoes instead of aubergines" was a "This England" item on 3 April 1964. The story about a woman taking her young son to watch hangings so that he could "learn right from wrong" appeared there on 2 June 1961. The item about a lodger not interrupting a murder "because he did not wish to be involved" had been picked up by the *New Statesman* on 16 January 1964. And so on. One can be almost certain that any quote in the book of an unintentionally funny item from a newspaper first had an airing in the *New Statesman*'s column of such oddities.

Since these "This England" items had also been used on the T.V. programme, anyone who was both a *Frost Report* viewer and a *New Statesman* reader, seeing them used for a third time in *To England With Love* might well have felt that so much mileage was being got out of them that the tread was starting to wear somewhat thin. Especially as early in 1968 an LP was brought out by Pye Records, called *The Frost Report on Everything*, and the same items were paraded all over again.

The point about all this borrowing was that, as everyone in the book-writing business knows, if you lift from only one source, that's plagiarism, but if you lift from two or more it's research. Nowhere in *To England With Love* did the co-authors go anywhere near approaching the classic example of borrowing some years ago by a Montreal sports writer. One morning when he had a crushing hangover he felt he just wouldn't be able to produce his column for that afternoon's paper. But he did manage to get one together. The first sentence read: "In his column in this morning's *New York Daily Mirror*, Grantland Rice said: . . ." He then reprinted the entire Rice column, and added a final sentence: "I'm inclined to agree with him."

The publishers of *To England With Love* (Heinemann with Hodder and Stoughton) felt that the reception it got from British book critics was "fairly hostile". An objective observer would go further than *fairly* hostile. Looking back over the reviews, one has to search diligently to build up any sort of body of friendly comment. The dominating mood was hostility. "Messrs. Frost and Jay obviously love everything that's old – old customs, old thoughts and old jokes." (*Sunday Telegraph*.) "Corn off the cob." (*Sunday Times*.) "Reads like a rapid series of instant last words." (*Times Literary Supplement*.) "The main effect of the book is to seem like an encyclopaedia of throw-away lines." (*Evening Standard*.) "Old jokes, of course, are the best jokes." (*Daily Telegraph*.) ". . . Ready butts for Frost to weigh in with his collection of hoary old jokes, apocryphal tales and interminable newspaper cuttings." (*Sheffield Morning Telegraph*.) "The funniest jokes tend to lose their point the second time round." (*Darlington Morning Echo*.)

Reading the book, one wonders where Frost leaves off and Jay takes over, or if in fact it should be the other way round. Frost says that at the Foyles' luncheon at which it sold more copies than any other book thus honoured, that it had been written by his writing a line and covering it up, then Jay writing a line and covering it, and so on. One of Hodder's editors said: "The best guide to who did what is to say that the bread and butter is by Jay and the jam by Frost."

But if this gives it something of the aura of a bit of "book-making", it was in fact a case of which came first the chicken or the egg. Frost has explained: "Tony Jay wrote some essays on various aspects of life in England and from these were evolved the format and content of *The Frost Report* series. Then afterwards we re-did the essays completely afresh in book form, and added twice as much again. I put the finishing touches to the book in a room at the Royal Station Hotel in Newcastle when I was doing a week up there at a club."

In contrast to the bad press the book had in England,

when it was published by Stein and Day in America as *The English* the critics were pretty ecstatic. All over the place, from the *New York Times* to the *Noblesville, Indiana, Ledger*. "Frost and Jay have produced one of the most delectable books of the season." (John Barkham, *Saturday Review Syndicate*.) "So amusing and mischievous that the impulse to quote at length is irresistible. As much fun to read as it must have been to write." (*Chicago Tribune*.) The reason for this enthusiasm was that the American critics differed from the English in that they came to it fresh. They had not heard the jokes before. *The Frost Report* had not been shown in America. Nor, for that matter, had *Not So Much a Programme* or any other series Frost has done since *That Was The Week*. Although his new series for Westinghouse has given him a bigger American television reputation, he was most widely known over there as "star of *That Was The Week*", the rather dated identification tag which was the most recognisable to Americans that publishers Stein and Day could use in their publicity.

The book stayed for months on the *New York Times* best-seller list and also the lists compiled by *Time, Book World* and *Publishers' Weekly*. The paperback rights were snapped up. MGM made an offer for television rights, an offer which was, as the publishers put it, "declined". Why declined? An intriguing situation, when you think about it.

The American sales of the book were helped considerably by Frost, in the three weeks prior to publication on 27 February 1968, making fifty-one television and radio appearances in New York, Philadelphia, Boston, Wash-

127

ington, Chicago, Cleveland and Hollywood, not to mention a clutch of literary luncheons, autograph parties and press receptions. At one autograph session he signed a hundred books in fifty minutes.

So successful was the promotion that 27 February has henceforth become a red letter day in Stein and Day's diary. They have announced: "27 February has now been designated as David Frost Day in the United States. On February next we expect to publish his new book." They were careful to avoid a clash with National Doughnut Week.

In 1961 when Frost had come down from Cambridge, writing – along with television and cabaret – was part of his triple assault on the big city. He had written for *Granta* and *Varsity*, the two university publications, and now he turned to Fleet Street and the magazines. Although the public is perhaps not conscious of it, he has by now been productive enough in this field of writing to require a whole drawer, labelled DAVID FROST: JOURNALISM, to be devoted to this aspect of his efforts in the bulging Frost filing cabinet in agent Diana Crawfurd's office.

A minor problem arose for Frost, budding writer, when it was realised that there was another David Frost in the business, a writer for *Autocar*. His by-line had been appearing for several years before the new Frost came on the scene and the motoring Frost wrote to the newcomer's agent suggesting he change his by-line to avoid confusion in the public mind. This sort of thing had happened before, notably in the case of a young Englishman some

128

With his Mercedes.

In his famous 'orange bomb' chair.

Frost conducts Julie Felix and Tom Lehrer at the
piano with the cast of *The Frost Report*

With Tory Leader, Edward Heath.

years ago who was establishing himself as a war correspondent and writer on other subjects when he received
a rather terse letter from America from Winston
Churchill saying that he was already a well established
author and the new man in the field should change his
name. Thus it is that *The History of the English-Speaking
Peoples* and other well-known books are by Winston S.
Churchill. In the case of the two Frosts, however, Diana
Crawfurd wrote a letter to the effect that they would
take their chances with the name as it stood and in the
event David Frost the second was considerably to out-
distance David Frost Mark I. Shortly after *To England
With Love* appeared in the bookshops yet another
David Frost, rugby football writer for the *Guardian*,
had a book out, about the 1967 All Blacks' tour of
Britain. Some booksellers displayed the two books side-
by-side, either in error or in the hope that some of the
gloss of the television Frost would rub off on the other.

The *Daily Mail* was one of the first to take an interest
in the young hopeful down from Cambridge and they
got him to do numerous features for them, ranging from
human interest pieces about the problems of fifteen-
year-old school leavers facing the big world to an interview with Billy Graham. He sold articles to *Town*,
Queen and the *Strand* and, interestingly enough, his
output included short stories.

His short stories were of the type known in the fiction
business as "mood pieces". A typical one, "Goodbye,
Mr. Gladston", concerned a passenger in a train who
noticed in a park they were passing an old man on a
bench giving sweets to children. Since the traveller always saw the old man there whenever he made that parti-

129

cular journey he was interested enough to find out who he was. He learned that he was an old out-of-work actor who timed his display of largesse to coincide with the passing of the express, so that the passengers would be suitably impressed. Parents, finding out about their youngsters accepting these gifts but not knowing the reason behind it, jumped to another conclusion and stopped their children from going near him, which hurt the old man deeply. This story appeared in the *Strand*, which is now defunct.

Frost's liking for writing and his desire to be known as a writer showed no falling off when *That Was The Week* involved him in the hurly-burly of television fame. With the programme at the height of its popularity in 1963, the *Observer* asked him to do a column for them and he readily accepted. His "Frost at Large" column, which ran for a year, consisted of his reflections on various aspects of the day, serious and amusing.

In 1964, when *Punch* were without a regular theatre critic following the death of Eric McKeown, Frost was given a three-month spell as their critic. Stage productions that he reviewed were as varied as *Inadmissable Evidence* ("The vigour of Osborne's writing has never been greater") and *Camelot*, which he felt had a pantomime atmosphere which made it difficult to get attuned to on its opening night in mid-summer – "When I was at school, early in August each year I would win three guineas from the local paper's 'Letter of the Week' column by sending them a few lines which began: 'Seen in a local store on the morning of August 4 – a display of Christmas cards. Surely Christmas is commercial enough already without . . .'" Alan Corren, Literary

Editor of *Punch*, says that the feeling around the office was that theatre criticism was not Frost's line. But Frost recalls how pleased he was that the Editor wanted him to do another stint for them.

In 1966 the *Spectator* got Frost to do their Press column for a period. At that time he not only had *The Frost Report* and its running mate *The Frost Programme* on his mind but also he was making so many flips back and forth to the States and the Continent that some of the columns had to be cabled from New York and France.

Around this time the *Sunday Express* approached him to do a column for them but he turned it down "because of embargoes". However, early in 1968 he signed to do a column for the *Sunday Mirror*, but what it was to be about, when it was to start and how he would find the time to write it were things which neither he, nor the Editor of the *Sunday Mirror*, were able to throw much light on as he emplaned yet again for New York immediately after the signing. It was hoped, however, that it would do something to further the reputation of David Frost, Columnist.

Frost has shared with others the difficulty a television personality turned columnist has in making any great impression on the public in the latter capacity. Bernard Braden, for example, when his *On the Braden Beat* television show ended was snapped up by the *Sun* to do a column for them, but such is the difference in impact between television and newspapers that not many people were aware that Braden was continuing to entertain the populace. It appears to work well around the other way, however. Bernard Levin, Clement Freud, Robert Pitman and other highly regarded and widely read newspaper columnists are able to augment their reputations by appearing on television. Odd that it doesn't work both ways.

The problem Frost has in fitting in the time for his writing has held up a project which for some years has been close to his heart. When he met a family which had played a big part in the Dutch Resistance during the war he was so enthralled by their story that he decided to write a book on them and the whole aspect of Holland's underground efforts against the Germans.

Ask his agent or his publishers when he will be finishing the Dutch Resistance book and they will say, "Ah, the Dutch Resistance book", the way a man will say, "Ah, the patio", whenever his wife asks him when he is going to build the long promised improvement to the garden. As a wit has remarked: "Frost will never get around to finishing *Thumbs in the Dyke*." Frost himself says: "I have set myself a delivery date of 1984."

It is difficult to think of anyone who has been able to combine authorship with full involvement in television. Norman Collins is the only one who comes readily to mind as a fully-fledged television man who has managed to produce what in the book world is called "a body of work" – *London Belongs To Me, Bond Street Story*, etc.. He did it by locking himself away with his typewriter from 11 p.m. to 3 a.m. each night when a book was on the boil. Writing is a lonely occupation and for those for whom it is not a full-time involvement it requires the self-discipline of cutting yourself off from the pre-occupations of your work and pleasant dallying with leisure friends to get down to it – alone. One finds it hard to picture Frost at any given time calling a halt to his obvious enjoyment of the television hurly-burly and his commitment to living life with all five senses at once, in order to say: "Sorry, got to go off to the old type-writer and get some more work done on the book."

He *is* starting to build up a body of work to the extent that he has another book to his credit besides *To England With Love*. It is called, in part, *How To Live Under Labour* and was a brilliant piece of "instant" publishing by live-wire Charles Pick of Heinemann. When the Frost satire fame was at its height in 1964, Pick got the idea of producing a scathing book on the Socialists if they got back into power in the election of that year. Frost, with Christopher Booker and Gerald Kaufman, was placed under starter's orders as the election got under way and the moment the result was known Pick notified the three of them: "We're in!" That was on 11 October 1964. Since Frost was com-muting between London and New York for his T.V. appearances, much of his contribution to the book had to be produced while he was airborne, as the printers realised when the pages of manuscript reached them headed, "B.O.A.C. Takes Good Care of You". Copies of the book were available on 17 November, which is undoubtedly a British record for the writing, printing and distribution of a book in a mere twenty-eight days. It contained some nice jibes at the Socialists ("Life in Tory Britain was everything on H.P. In Labour Britain it will be H.P. on everything") and sold so well that even Heinemann themselves can't now find a spare copy.

But as with *To England With Love* it was a shared book in respect of Frost authorship. Undeniably there were good cracks in it but no indication as to which were Frost's, which Booker's, and which Kaufman's.

Two other pieces of book-making complete the present library of Frost's work between covers, hard and soft.

In 1963 W. H. Allen published a beautifully produced book titled *That Was The Week That Was*, edited by David Frost and Ned Sherrin. A pleasure to handle, it contains the cream of the T.V. show's scripts, with artwork by the late, very popular Timothy Birdsall and others. For a new generation not old enough to have seen *TW3* on the screen, the pace is set in the book with the words written above the title: "In the beginning God created the heaven and the earth . . . and on the seventh day God ended his work which he had made; and he rested on the seventh day from all his work which he had made . . . THAT WAS THE WEEK THAT WAS."

In 1967, Cornmarket Press published *Playback: 1*, transcripts of the best interviews of the first series of *The Frost Programme*. Strangely, it did not have a good sale and the publishers have no firm plans for *Playback: 2*. It is hard to understand why it was not a success, since it has such interviews as those with George Brown, the Archbishop of Canterbury, Mick Jagger, Ian Smith and Lord Thomson and it makes good reading to study at leisure what was caught fleetingly on the television screen. Frost's explanation of why it was not a success was that "it was in magazine format and people thought *Playback* was a magazine they had never heard of."

Frost's ardent desire to be known as an author is

quite understandable. Although his agent says that appearing on television is his adrenalin, he needs nothing more, anyone who has appeared on television knows that it is not enough. It gives you a great feeling, having yourself on display before several million unseen viewers. But when it is all over, what have you got to show for it? It is ephemeral. The satisfaction to be derived from having a book published is a continuing thing. A book is tangible. You can hold it in your hands. You can give copies to your friends. You can autograph it. You can't autograph a television appearance.

When Frost does get around to writing a book which he can justifiably call "all my own work" it will be good. But if he manages to fit it in with his present heavy commitment as television star, impresario and businessman it will be surprising.

Chapter 9

Whither Frost?

Where does Frost go from here?

When the question was put to John Wells, of *Private Eye*, he said: "David cannot help but go into politics." Paul Foot, who occupies a desk adjoining Wells, hastened to comment: "To put a quick stop to such a possibility, Frost should be made a peer at once."

When Frost himself was asked, "What do you expect to be doing when you're forty?" he said: "I think I know but I'm damned if I'm going to tell anybody now."

The view of Muriel Brightwell, perceptive wife of Frost's production manager, was: "I think you will find that David will concentrate more and more on business. He loves business management."

She could possibly be right. Frost, increasingly immersed in business, might soon be spending far more time in the board room than in the studio. "Business is a bore to many people," *The Times* admitted, in what can only be taken as explanation of why so many copies of its business section are to be seen in their discarded, pristine state in living rooms and hotel lobbies up and down the country. When one starts to look into Frost the businessman he becomes a less interesting person, so perhaps it is as well not to dwell too long on this aspect. But when one works one's way through the

136

details of his business activities, it is found that there *is* a bonus. The story of how the Frost consortium got London Weekend Television is fascinating.

Frost's main business interests, at time of going to press, consisted of:

David Paradine Ltd.,
David Paradine Productions Ltd.,
Television Advisers Ltd.,
Clive Irving Ltd.,
David Paradine Documentaries Ltd.,
London Weekend Television.

David Paradine Ltd., the first company he formed, was the simple expedient of turning yourself into a company for tax reasons as soon as you start doing well. It hires out David Frost to television, cabaret, the theatre and anyone else who wants his services as a performer.

David Paradine Productions Ltd., which is run for Frost by George Brightwell, originates and develops properties for sale to television networks, film companies and the theatre. It was David Paradine Productions, for instance, which negotiated the $300,000 contract with Westinghouse of America for their *David Frost Presents* series.

Brightwell, one of the few people in the immediate vicinity of Frost who is of an age that he can talk about his war experiences, was for thirteen years Controller of Forces' Entertainment Services and then after seven years as Programme Administrator with A.B.C. Television he linked up with Frost. That was in 1966, when Brightwell met him through being production manager

137

for Frost's *Night Out in London,* a show done for the American Broadcasting Corporation network.

The first shows that David Paradine Productions have, so far, got on to the airwaves have been *At Last the 1948 Show, No – That's Me Over Here* and *The Ronnie Barker Playhouse,* which have brought up to star status the trio of supporting players from *The Frost Report* – John Cleese, and the Ronnies Corbett and Barker.

Frost has been billed as Executive Producer, which suggests in the public mind that he is actively engaged in getting each show on the air. But, in point of fact, he merely devises and supervises them at the birth pangs stage and leaves it to Brightwell and each production team to see things through under his overall direction. "He is good at delegating," says Brightwell. "He doesn't breath down the back of your neck all the time. Once he has confidence in you and you're on the job for him, he leaves you to it."

The question was put to Brightwell: "For Frost to have achieved all he has done while still in his twenties, what is really left for him, what challenge is there?"

"There is plenty left for him," said Brightwell. "What about films? He is very keen on films, but hasn't done much about them yet."

"Or the theatre, presumably."

"No, not the theatre. That's different. That doesn't have such pressing interest for David. You make a different sort of reputation in the theatre. More limited, not like the mass audiences of television and films. If I were asked to put in a nutshell what I think is David's aim, I would say it is to get the same recognition in the world as he has achieved in this country."

James Gilbert, producer of *The Frost Report*, has said that "going steely-eyed" was the nearest he had ever seen Frost get to losing his temper and when Brightwell, who works as closely with Frost as anybody, was asked whether he had ever known him to lose his temper, Brightwell's secretary was at her desk in the room and in unison they said, "Once!" Asked whether they would relate the incident, they said they would prefer not to. Subsequent research failed to bring to light where and when the unique blow-up had occurred but, judging by how firmly it was imprinted on their minds, one felt that it must have been spectacular.

Brightwell and secretary Joan Grimwade's office is in Denmark Street, London's Tin Pan Alley, and the Frost expansion is reflected in the fact that they used to work from Frost's home. Other Frost interests are housed elsewhere and the plan now is to combine them all in one big office. Coming soon – The Frost Building?

Television Advisers Ltd., of which Frost is a director, are a firm of close circuit consultants. The company, of which Iain Macleod is Chairman, was started in 1963 with a capital of £100 by Wynford Vaughan Thomas, former B.B.C. man and now Programme Director of Harlech Television. Their operations are conducted mainly at sales conferences and advertising promotions for industry, and they have an annual turnover in excess of £100,000.

Clive Irving has gone from success to success in the magazine world, apart from a couple of setbacks, and he gets top billing in an enterprise of which Frost has a large share, Clive Irving Ltd., a company brought into being to explore all sorts of possibilities in the field of periodicals in particular and publishing in general. Richard Ingrams, editor of *Private Eye*, wonders what sort of magazines Frost will spawn. He tells of going on a train trip with Frost. "I bought *New Statesman, Spectator*, that sort of thing, and I was a bit surprised to see David settle down in a corner with *Melody Maker*. I had never actually seen anybody reading it."

The newly formed David Paradine Documentaries Ltd. has Antony Jay as Frost's co-director. As its name suggests, it will produce films for industry and education. Frost is hopeful that it will bring a certain freshness to this in-a-rut branch of movie making by the use of the production and performing talents of top television people.

Which now brings us to what so far has been the high-water mark of Frost's excursion into the world of big business – London Weekend Television.

How did David Frost and his associates manage to snatch the juiciest plum in commercial television – London weekends? In fact, how does one go about forming a consortium to apply for a television franchise and, even more important, make a successful application? Piecing together the various accounts of the people involved, this was the Frost method . . .

Towards the end of 1966, people who were interested in such things began to formulate plans to bid for the franchises which were to be renewed or re-allocated by the Independent Television Authority as of July 1968.

There were fourteen existing stations and there was to be the addition of a fifteenth – Yorkshire.

Apart from possibilities down in Wales, the feeling was that none of the companies "in residence" could be dislodged. There might be a reshuffle of the big boys – A.B.C., Rediffusion, A.T.V. and Granada – who had the most lucrative areas (London, Midlands and the North) nicely carved up among themselves. But getting a franchise away from them was regarded as pretty well impossible.

So – the focal point was Yorkshire, where it would be every man for himself in the attempt to get the nod from the I.T.A..

Frost, however, felt that if one were to have an effect on television one must do it from the centre, from London, rather than out in Yorkshire.

"I was thinking about it a lot," he relates. "At a Rediffusion staff party at the Lyceum, in the first week of January 1967, there were lots of jokes about the Yorkshire franchise and as I came away I thought more about the chances in London. I remember later that night phoning Clive Irving and saying: 'It has to be London weekend.'

"I felt it would be possible to make out a case if you had the strongest possible television group of people and started a company that way round. In other words, *start* with the television people because it is a television company and then find the compatible finance, rather than setting up a finance company that just happens to go into television instead of, say, soap. The basic way the original independent companies had been formed was that shrewd and brave businessmen got together

141

and then hired television people to sit in on the running of the actual programmes. I felt that changing the procedure around would be a good basis for an application, one that could appeal to the I.T.A.

"Having outlined this to Clive, the next person I talked to about it was someone who was to become a valued member of our group – Peter Hall. It was on the night the B.B.C. did a repeat of *Cathy Come Home*. I had an item in my programme about it and the discussion became so interesting that it went on to monopolise the whole programme. Peter Hall was supposed to appear on another topic but he had to be left out, and we went off together afterwards. The London consortium idea wasn't fully worked out in my mind yet and I hadn't decided finally what to do. I talked vaguely about it to him and he reacted at once: 'As far as I'm concerned,' he said, 'if you decide to do it, then count me in.' His simple reaction was in effect the deciding factor. If people like Peter Hall would go along with me, I realised it was on."

Having given himself the green light, Frost got down to the detailed planning. First, to assemble the group of television people . . . Humphrey Burton, Doreen Stephens, Michael Peacock, John Freeman . . . good, solid television names.

John Freeman, who had been a T.V. personality when Frost was still a schoolboy, was now Ambassador to India but coming up for a change of scene. Frost flew out there ("a day trip to India") and Freeman proved enthusiastic. But other things were in the offing. Instead of embracing the prospect of returning to television as a top executive, Freeman finally decided in favour of the

142

perhaps more important role of Ambassador to the United States.

Aidan Crawley was among those planning to go after the new Yorkshire franchise. Crawley, highly respected Conservative M.P. for West Derbyshire, former county cricketer, founder of Independent Television News and otherwise very experienced T.V. man, was the perfect Chairman figure. Yes, he said, he would switch his sights from Yorkshire to London and join with Frost. Michael Peacock, former head of B.B.C.1 had talked at an earlier stage with Crawley about going to Yorkshire but had swung round to preferring Frost's idea of going for London weekends and of his being Managing Director. The fact that Crawley was now joining the London bid suited him admirably.

The obvious thing would have been for Frost to fit himself in there on the prospective Board, but under the terms of the Television Act no director of an independent company could also be a performer for that company. For Frost, the thought of coming off the screen to appear on the letterhead was "ludicrous". So he would merely have an equity in the consortium and officially be no more than an "adviser".

When the other television men were settled upon, Frost turned, at the beginning of February 1967, to the financial side of the enterprise.

"The first businessman I approached was Arnold Weinstock of G.E.C. and the next was Sir Donald Stokes of Leyland Motors. Then there was Duncan McNab of the London Co-operative Society and the Hon. David Montagu of Samuel Montagu the bankers."

143

"How did you approach these men – by letter, through an intermediary?"

"I phoned them."

"You mean you just picked up the phone and said to Arnold Weinstock: 'I'm forming a consortium to bid for London Weekend Television. Would you care to join us?'"

"In effect, yes."

"And what was his reaction?"

"Arnold's reaction was delightful. He said that as G.E.C. manufacture T.V. sets he had an interest in television fascinating people more than it was at the moment and therefore it was in his direct interests to encourage the group."

"That was his immediate reaction?"

"More or less immediate. I arranged to have lunch with each of them after giving them an initial outline of my plans on the phone."

"Did any turn you down?"

"Two or three thought it was 'a lovely idea' but checked with people they knew, who they thought were authorities on what the I.T.A. would do, and came back with the news that it was impossible. Of course, I didn't tell the others about these ones who had turned it down. After all, these backers were going into it as a thousand-to-one chance."

"How did those who hadn't gone along with you feel when you got it?"

"Several of them phoned me the day after it came through and said, 'David . . . er . . . I've been thinking things over and perhaps . . .' I had to tell them I was sorry but in our application we had to be definite as to

144

who all our backers were and it was too late to add any others."

Deadline for applications had been April 15 and with the television personnel and the financial backers settled by the end of February, Frost and his colleagues entered a hectic period of six weeks of staff work, with meeting after meeting at his home, at the home of Aidan Crawley in nearby Chester Square, in the board room of G.E.C., at Samuel Montagu the bankers.

The I.T.A. had made it clear that they would not entertain any bid for London's weekends that didn't have £6,000,000 behind it, since they obviously could not risk a company that was not firmly based financially getting the franchise.

The consortium decided that to go through, with the basis that it was television expertise with finance built around it, thirty per cent of the equity must be reserved for the creators and administrators of television. So, of the £1,500,000 of equity, some £500,000 must go to the people who were actually going to be involved. The other £1,000,000 went to the backers – the financial interests who had to be prepared to put up three times as much as that in loan stock if required. So the financial structure wound up as a million plus three million – £4,000,000 – from the backers, plus the half million "creative" equity, plus bank overdraft facilities with Barclays for another £2,000,000, making £6,500,000 in all – half a million more than was needed.

The I.T.A. gave guidance to those making applications, in the form of a list of categories in which they wanted to know such things as who was in the consortium, what it stood for, what its policy was, the pre-cise framework of its finances.

"As far as the financial side was concerned this was primarily looked after by David Montagu, of the bankers, and Peat Marwick, the accountants, who worked closely with Michael Peacock. They did a fan-tastic job in sorting out the figures. The sort of detail wanted from us was how much we would be spending on electric typewriters three years hence. Well, really! This, with all the strictly television aspects of the applica-tion, meant that in the end it became an eighty-page document."

"Did you feel that you had to put some salesmanship into it?"

"No. It was almost a point of paring that out, so that it was a straight recital of facts and policy. We tried to avoid sales jargon. We felt it was irrelevant. And we didn't publicise the consortium. It was important not to put any pressure on anybody. We did the whole thing in private; the only announcement of the existence of the London weekend consortium, the first time the story broke, was in a press release by the B.B.C.. When they announced that Michael Peacock was leaving the cor-poration they mentioned that he was doing so to join us – and then, of course, the papers jumped on to it."

The neatly bound volume of eighty pages of foolscap typescript was delivered by hand, as per instructions, to the I.T.A. on 15 April 1967, and then it was a matter of Frost and Co. waiting to learn when they would be called for the interview.

It was a wait of three weeks before they were sum-moned to I.T.A. headquarters in the Brompton Road, almost opposite Harrods. Seven members of the consortium presented themselves – Frost, Crawley, Peacock, Irving, Montague, Dr. Tom Margerison and Ian Bowey, representing the accountants and there to vouch for the figures.

The interview had been called for 11 a.m. and their natural feeling of being somewhat on edge was not helped by the fact that they had to sweat it out in the waiting room for fifty minutes until the preceding interview was finished. At length they were ushered in, to find Lord Hill, then Chairman of the I.T.A., and the twelve other Members, seated at tables placed together to form one big table in the shape of an open square. Facing this was a long table for the visitors, with place cards before each chair, so that they would know, banquet style, where to sit.

The interview lasted for just over an hour, during which time probing questions were asked about programming, money matters, any aspect that any of the Members chose to pick upon in the document. Then Lord Hill asked Frost and Crawley, as joint Chairmen of the consortium, to make a short concluding speech before the proceedings came to an end.

When Frost was asked how it felt being at the interview he said: "We didn't quite know how to feel. None of us had ever had a similar experience. There is no other set-up quite like that, so what do you compare it to?"

"Were you looking for indications in anything they said?"

"Good heavens, yes. It was possible to take anything, like 'Good morning', and weigh up in your mind

147

whether the way they said it was a good omen or not. But one thing that seemed hopeful was that the questions were serious and practical, which could have indicated that they were interested in approving our application . . . and then it could have meant merely that they were being polite and covering up the fact that we had no chance at all."

"What did you do afterwards?"

"We went and had lunch at the Hyde Park Hotel. Nobody could think of anything where we had gone greatly wrong but also nobody could say how right it had gone. It was a subdued affair, that lunch."

Then followed a wait that was longer and more agonising than the time-lag between delivering the application and having the interview, because now they were waiting for the verdict. The I.T.A. decisions on the new constitution of the independent stations was to be made public by Monday, 12 June. It was thought probable that those who applied would be told at the weekend, to avoid the stock market being affected.

"Did you put out feelers during this waiting period, to see whether you could get a tip-off?"

"Naturally we made discreet enquiries of anybody we thought might have a clue. But nobody knew. It was a tremendous achievement by the I.T.A.. The security was total."

On the Saturday morning Frost stopped off at Newmarket on his way to Beccles to visit his mother and had a chat with David Montagu.

"He was depressed about the outcome. I tried to reassure him – with absolutely nothing to go on. Then, that night, Lord Hill phoned asking us to show ourselves

at I.T.A. headquarters next morning. This was it! But
Michael Peacock was down in Cornwall on holiday and
we couldn't locate him, so he was to miss out on the
final act. Well, not the *final* act. The end of the first act.

"Aidan, David Montagu, Tom Margerison and I duly
arrived at I.T.A. headquarters and just as we got there
Lord Derby was coming out. He looked black. We
didn't know until later that T.W.W. had lost their franchise. But Paul Adorian, Managing Director of Rediffusion, drove up as we were going in and we did sense
that everybody was being told that morning, one after
the other. A somewhat brutal procession, but how else
could it have been done?

"Lord Hill was quite unemotional when he gave us
the verdict, just read from a piece of paper. We were
in! It was subject to certain conditions but we were
only too glad to go along with those. The main condition
was that we include papers in our group, ones that had
missed out elsewhere – the *Telegraph*, *Observer* and
Economist. I.T.A. felt that it was good to have newspapers represented."

"Did you have a celebration?"

"We drove to my house to pick up Clive Irving. Poor
Clive, he had had a terrible couple of hours sitting there
stewing while we were getting the decision. Then we
collected Virginia, Aidan Crawley's delightful wife, and
we all went and had a dazed lunch at the Ritz."

"Dazed? Weren't you elated?"

"That had come earlier, immediately after we got the
good news. I remember somebody at lunch saying that
it was like when you get all keyed up applying for some
big job and then, when you get it, after the first flush of

149

excitement comes the reality, and the responsibility, when you say to yourself: 'Now I have to deliver.' "

And has London Weekend Television delivered? Does the setting up of an independent T.V. company on the basis of thinking of the television personnel first, and the financial people second, produce better television or does it just come out very much the mixture as before? This final verdict is now, of course, in the hands of the most important group of all – the viewers.

There is the true story of Lord Thomson in his Mr. Thomson days in Canada when he was at a luncheon and someone indicated the man sitting on the other side of him. "I don't believe you've met Mr. So-and-So, Roy. He owns the *Blanksville Gazette*." Roy Thomson turned to him. "Want to sell it?"

Frost, although becoming more and more interested in business, has not yet reached the obsession stage. The signs are not there yet that it will completely overshadow his liking for being the performer. You can still put on a pretty good performance in the board room. But the audience is not large enough. It does not seem probable that he will lightly throw away all the personal satisfaction readily to be gained by appearing before his huge, unseen audience.

Diana Crawfurd has said: "David is a child of the television age. Appearing on television is his adrenalin."

Concrete, though merely hinted at, proof of the continuing story of Frost the performer came when he was setting off on yet another flight to the United States after his Presidential programme had been screened. A newspaperman asked him what he was up to next. "I can't say," he replied with a smile, "but you can make another of your shrewd guesses by saying that I'm going to become much more involved in American television."

To be lost to public gaze behind office walls would mean denying himself the immense pleasure to be derived from having fans. Such as the window cleaner who poked his head in through the window when Frost was having a programme conference at his home, to say: "Good on you – taking the mickey out of the Top Brass. It's nice to know you're one of Us against Them." Or the virile young man who, when told that the Frost show was going to be switched from weekdays to weekends, said: "Dammit. That's going to ruin my courting."

And there is another reason why Frost might deem it unwise at this point to put all his eggs in the business basket. Freddie Ross has said: "The thing about showbiz is that it is just what it says – one side is 'show' and the other 'biz'. On the show side are the performers, and on the other are the impresarios and the financial boys. Some people graduate from the one side to the other. Jack Hylton was the big example of this. They are tough cookies over there on the biz side and one wonders whether David is going to be taken. He is there with them now on the strength of the fact that he is 'David Frost'. But without the booming market as far as David Frost the performer is concerned, would he still be acceptable to the big boys on the business side? Can David really stack up against them on business acumen alone? He has integrity, morality and loyalty. It could destroy him."

Frost is indeed the hottest property in television at

the moment and the outcome of this is that he has
hangers-on the way other people have mice. Not only
artistes, writers and ideasmen who work for him, or
want to, but also television executives who work with
him, or want to. Not all the latter are bright. As Tom
Ferguson, arts editor of the *Sunday Telegraph*, says: "I
have never met so many nits in high places as I have in
television." But the point is that they are *experienced*
nits. They know the routine and the technicalities of
television. If one would have ideal confrères it would
be necessary to select talented young likeables and bring
them on, which would all take too long; it is expedient
to settle for those who know the ropes, even if it is about
all they do know. Constantly they hover around Frost.
They are not very rewarding company. How he puts up
with them, day in, night out, Frost alone knows.

But on his list of Things To Do he is coming up to
the item "Get Married", and then he won't need to
spend so much time with them.

If one were writing a profile on Frost and came to
sum him up, this is probably what one would say of
him:

He is the best television interviewer in the country.
He has brought interviewing to such a fine art that he
makes Robin Day, Michelmore and their ilk look good
only sometimes, Eamonn Andrews never. Robin Day,
the master, who wrote a book about T.V. interviewing
before Frost even entered television, could well learn
from the pupil. Day is always aggressive; Frost adjusts
to his subject.

He is dedicated to making television a more worth-while thing. "One has to decide whether television is to be Stimulant or Sleeping Pill. If it is going to be merely the Horlicks of the mind, we might as well pack up. The aim of every T.V. programme I do is to leave the audience a little more aware, a little more alert, a little more alive."

As a person he is thoroughly likeable. Kind, generous, thoughtful of others. There is something almost saintly about him. He is either a good advertisement for Methodism or else it is just how he happens to be.

But he is not a prig. He does not look with disapproval on drinking, smoking and sex, though he has no great interest in the first two.

In conversation he tends to make too frequent use of certain phrases. The three currently being overworked: "in this area", by which he means "in this regard"; "at this moment in time", by which he means "now"; and "Good good good good good!", by which he means "Good!"

He is articulate but not profound. If you go to a newspaper clippings library and delve through the Frost folders, which will be numerous, you will find little that is quotable out of the mouth of Frost. Peter Cook has said: "David has his platform for the future all worked out, but he doesn't quite know what he's going to say on it."

He is completely self-assured, but not brash. Where other young people in their twenties might hesitate to phone the Prime Minister, the Pope or the President of the United States, Frost will do so without giving it a second thought, because he feels they will be just as interested as he is in what he wants to talk to them about. And it is almost certain that they will be. He overflows with infectious exuberance. George Brightwell says: "Whenever David phones to tell me something he's excited about I always feel I've had my batteries recharged."

The dominant trait in his character is ambition. In the words of Elkan Allan, the man who came in at the beginning, the one who gave him his first chance in television: "David is the most ambitious person I have ever met or heard of. There is no limit to where his ambition will take him. President of the first World Government, that's it! You may think I'm joking but I really feel David's ambition is to be President of the first World Government. And I think he'll make it."